War Stories

THE AMERICAN CIVIL WAR, REMEMBERED BY THOSE WHO WERE THERE

Mark Weaver

AmericanCivilWarStory.com

Mark Weaver/AmericanCivilWarStory.com
mark@americancivilwarstory.com
www.americancivilwarstory.com

Book Layout ©2013 BookDesignTemplates.com

Ordering Information:
Quantity sales. Special discounts are available on quantity purchases by corporations, associations, and others. For details, contact the "Special Sales Department" at the email address above.

War Stories/Mark Weaver. —1st ed.
ISBN-13: 978-1499650235

Book Cover Design by Kashif Ford:
(http://www.fiverr.com/fordkashif/create-an-awesome-book-cover-for-you)

Front cover portraits: (clockwise from top left) Robert Smalls (pg. 47), Phillip Sheridan (pg. 131), John Mosby (pg. 147), and Phoebe Pember (pg. 209).

Contents

Author's Introduction 1

CHAPTER ONE 5

  A Student of the Art of Foraging 6

  The Battle of Shiloh 9

  The Fate of a Prisoner of War 20

CHAPTER TWO 27

  The View from the CSS Virginia (Merrimac) 28

  The View from the USS Monitor 40

CHAPTER THREE 47

  Robert Smalls 47

  Hanged as a Spy 55

  A Nurse Turned Spy 65

CHAPTER FOUR 79

  Prelude to Battle 80

  The Attack 91

  Defeat, Regrouping, and Counter-attacking 101

CHAPTER FIVE 109

A General Set Adrift 110

Anti-Aircraft Fire 115

The Confederate Aeronaut............................. 118

CHAPTER SIX 131

Foraging Party Makes a Surprising Discovery 132

The Battle of Stones River 134

In Search of a Comfortable Way to Travel.............. 144

CHAPTER SEVEN... 147

The Ride around McClellan 148

Birth of a Partisan................................... 153

The "Greenback" Raid................................. 166

A Meeting with Mosby................................. 171

CHAPTER EIGHT 181

Joining the Army of the Potomac 181

Foraging... 187

New Recruits.. 191

Picket Duty 194

Battle 198

CHAPTER NINE 209

The First Day 210

Writing A Letter 214

Hiring Some Help 216

The Whiskey Barrel 221

Union Occupation 225

CHAPTER TEN 229

A Final Act Of Respect 230

The Final Charge 233

The Final Day 235

The Final Story 243

Thank you to my intrepid proofreaders. Who, among other things, brought me to a better understanding of the difference between the plural and past tenses.

Here, in the dread tribunal of last resort, valor contended against valor. Here brave men struggled and died for the right as God gave them to see the right.
— ADLAI E. STEVENSON I

Author's Introduction

I am not a historian. I am just someone who loves learning all I can about history. There is so much great history that is never taught in schools, and if you don't look for yourself you might never realize what you are missing.

The history of the American Civil War is no different. You may think you know quite a bit about this important part of American History, but there is a good chance that there are many facets of it you know little about.

That is why I put this book together. While I have been doing research for AmericanCivilWarStory.com, I have come across so many cool stories that I had never heard before. What is even better, many of these stories were written by the people who actually lived them. Finally, I decided to collect some of my favorites into a book so that everyone could enjoy these great Civil War Stories.

One thing to keep in mind when reading these stories is that most people remember things the way they want to. Usually putting themselves in the best light possible, and those who wrote about their Civil War experiences were no different. When Union General William T. Sherman wrote his memoirs, many people found fault with the way he presented his story. So, in the preface to the second edition of his memoirs he included the following paragraph:

> *"In this free country every man is at perfect liberty to publish his own thoughts and impressions, and any witness who may differ from me should publish his own version of facts in the truthful narration of which he is interested. I am publishing my own memoirs, not theirs, and we all know that no three honest witnesses of a simple brawl can agree on all the details. How much more likely will be the difference in a great battle covering a vast space of broken ground, when each division, brigade, regiment, and even company, naturally and honestly believes that it was the focus of the whole affair! Each of them won the battle. None ever lost. That was the fate of the old man who unhappily commanded."*

There are even some stories in this book that contain statements in direct contradiction of each other (Ex: The stories about the Battle of Hampton Roads contain more than one contradiction). The point is that these are the stories of the people who were actually there, living and dying for their cause in the Civil War. The stories you will read are their war stories, and I hope you enjoy hearing them firsthand as much as I did.

Some notes on how this book is put together, each chapter contains an introduction from me, and I introduce each story within the chapter as well. Everything written by me will be in italics (Ex: *Chapter introductions written by me*). I have done some editing of the original texts, where there were obvious mistakes by the printer, but I tried to leave the original writings much as the authors wrote them. You will find misspellings, old fashioned spellings, unfamiliar words, and even some bad grammar; but I felt they added authenticity so I mostly left them as I found them. I have removed some sections either to remove unrelated or unimportant details, or simply to shorten stories to fit in the book. Where I have removed paragraphs or sentences from the original text it is indicated with an ellipsis (Ex: ...).

Thanks for taking the time to read War Stories, and I hope you will enjoy this book.

CHAPTER ONE

ALL THE OPPOSING ARMIES OF GREY AND BLUE
FIERCELY BLAZED AT EACH OTHER

— HENRY MORTON STANLEY —

O n January 28, 1841, a young unmarried woman in the
Welsh county of Denbighshire had a son. He was named
John Rowlands. John's mother abandoned her newborn
son, and his grandfather took him in. Unfortunately, his grandfather died when John was only five years old, and the young boy was
eventually sent to a workhouse for the poor where he was raised
until the age of fifteen.

At the age of eighteen, young Mr. Rowlands took passage on a
ship bound for the United States; and in 1859, he began a new life in
New Orleans, Louisiana. Here the story gets a bit murky...

Once in New Orleans, John got a job with a local grocery whole-
saler, James Speake. According to John, he got the job on the recommendation of a wealthy cotton merchant who had taken a liking to
him, Henry Hope Stanley. James Speake soon died, and John claims
that Mr. Stanley took him in, treated him as a son, and renamed
him Henry Stanley. Modern historians disagree. Citing many incon-
sistencies in his diaries and writings, historians have concluded that
Mr. Rowlands took the name Henry Stanley in honor of the success-

ful merchant; but that his relationship with the man was not very close or possibly even non-existent.

Whatever the case, by the beginning of the Civil War, in 1861, our young hero was working in a grocery store in Cyprus Bend, Arkansas, under the name Henry Stanley. It wouldn't be until after the war that he would add the middle name "Morton." Nevertheless, the famed explorer of Africa, the man who coined the phrase, "Dr. Livingston, I presume," Sir Henry Morton Stanley had found his name.

The winds of war were blowing in young Mr. Stanley's Arkansas home; and whether he knew it or not, he was going to play a part in the coming conflict. Following are some stories[1] from his service in the Civil War.

A Student of the Art of Foraging

Early in the war, our young hero enlisted as a Confederate volunteer in a local company called the "Dixie Greys." He did not enlist from some burning desire to make war; but rather, he wished to avoid being called a coward by any pretty young ladies in the area.

Like most of the soldiers in both armies early in the war, Stanley had no notion of what war really was; but he was about to find out. One of his first lessons was an introduction to the finer points of the soldier's shadowy art of "foraging"...

The long halt at Cave City served to initiate me into the mysteries of foraging, which, in army-vocabulary, meant not only to steal from the enemy, but to exploit Secessionist sympathisers, and obtain for love and money some trifles to make life more enjoyable. Malone and Slate were very successful and

---

[1] Taken from *The Autobiography of Sir Henry Morton Stanley*, edited by Dorothy Stanley, 1909.

clever in all sorts of ruses. I was envious of the praises given to them, and resolved to outdo them. What rackings of the brain I suffered, as I mentally revolved the methods to adopt! General Sidney Johnston gave not so much time to the study of inflicting defeat on the Yankees, as I gave to win glory from the mess by my exploits. Half-a-dozen times in December it had been my turn to forage, but, somehow, my return was not greeted with any rapturous applause. However, by Christmas Eve I had a fair knowledge of the country and the temper of the people about, and my mind was stored with information regarding Secessionists, Unionists, and lanes, and farms, to a radius of five miles around the camp. Just on the edge of my circle, there lay one fat farm towards Green River, the owner of which was a Yank, and his neighbour told me he corresponded with the enemy. For a foot-soldier, the distance was somewhat far, but for a horse- man, it was nothing.

The day before Christmas, through the assistance of a man named Tate, I had the promise of a mule; and having obtained the countersign from Armstrong, I set out, as soon as it was dark, to levy a contribution on the Unionist farmer. It was about ten o'clock by the time I reached the place. Tying my mule in the angle of a fence, I climbed over, and explored the grounds. In crossing a field, I came to half-a-dozen low mounds, which I was certain contained stores of potatoes, or something of the kind. I burrowed into the side of one of them with my bayonet, and presently I smelled apples. These were even better than potatoes, for they would do splendidly for dumplings. I half-filled a sack with them. After burrowing into two or three others, I came to one which contained the winter store of potatoes, and I soon raked out enough to make a load. I hurried with my booty to my mule, and secured it on the mule.

Then, thinking that a goose, or even a duck or a fowl or two, would make our Christmas dinner complete, I was tempted to make a quest for them, anticipating, as I crept towards the farm, the glory I should receive from my mess. I reached the out-houses with every faculty strained, and I soon had the pleasure of wringing the neck of a goose, a duck, and two fowls.

I ought to have had the discretion to retire now, but the ambition to extinguish Malone and Slate, to see the grin of admiration on Armstrong's face, and Newton Story open his eyes, and Tomasson compelled to pay homage to worth, left me still dissatisfied; and just then scenting a hog-pen, I quietly moved towards it. By the light of a feeble moon I worked into the piggies' home, and there, cuddled about the hams of their mother, I saw the pinky forms of three or four plump shoats. Aye, a tender shoat, roasted brown and crisp, would be the crown of a Christmas dinner! I bounded lightly as a lean fox into the sty, snatched a young porkling up by the heels, creating a terrifying clamour by the act. We were all alarmed, the mother hoarsely grunted, the piggies squealed in a frightful chorus, the innocent rent the midnight air with his cries; but, determined not to lose my prize, I scrambled over, ended its fears and struggles by one fierce slash, dumped the carcase into the sack, and then hastened away. Lights were visible in the farm-house, doors slammed, and by a broad beam of light I saw a man in the doorway with a gun in his hand. A second later a shower of pellets whistled about me, fortunately without harm, which sent me tearing madly towards my mule. In a few minutes, bathed in perspiration, I was astride of my mule, with my sack of dead meat in front of me, and potatoes and apples thumping the sides of my animal as I rode away towards camp.

Long before dawn, I made my triumphant appearance in front of my tent, and was rewarded by every member of the mess with the most grateful acknowledgements. The Christmas dinner was a splendid success, and over twenty invited guests sat down to it, and praises were on every lip; but without the apple dumplings and fritters it would not have been complete to us youngsters. Secretly, I was persuaded that it was as wrong to rob a poor Unionist as a Secessionist; but the word 'foraging,' which, by general consent, was bestowed on such deeds, mollified my scruples. Foragers were sent out by the authorities every other day, and even authorised to seize supplies by force; and, according to the military education I was receiving, I did not appear to be so very wicked as my conscience was inclined to make me out to be.

The Battle of Shiloh

In early April 1862, Stanley would learn what war was truly all about. In the early morning hours of April 6th, the Dixie Greys took part in a surprise attack on the Union forces camped around Pittsburg Landing on the Tennessee River. This is Stanley's account of the Battle of Shiloh and the lasting impression it made on him...

Henry Morton Stanley, in 1890.

Day broke with every promise of a fine day. Next to me, on my right, was a boy of seventeen, Henry Parker. I remember it because, while we stood-at-ease, he drew my attention to some violets at his feet, and said, 'It would be a good idea to put a few into my cap. Perhaps the Yanks won't shoot me if they see me wearing such flowers, for they are a sign of peace.' 'Capital,' said I, 'I will do the same.' We plucked a bunch, and arranged the violets in our caps. The men in the ranks laughed at our proceedings, and had not the enemy been so near, their merry mood might have been communicated to the army.

...

'Forward, gentlemen, make ready!' urged Captain Smith. In response, we surged forward, for the first time marring the alignment. We trampled recklessly over the grass and young sprouts. Beams of sunlight stole athwart our course. The sun was up above the horizon. Just then we came to a bit of pack-land, and overtook our skirmishers, who had been engaged in exploring our front. We passed beyond them. Nothing now stood between us and the enemy.

'There they are!' was no sooner uttered, than we cracked into them with levelled muskets. 'Aim low, men!' commanded Captain Smith. I tried hard to see some living thing to shoot at, for it appeared absurd to be blazing away at shadows. But, still advancing, firing as we moved, I, at last, saw a row of little globes of pearly smoke streaked with crimson, breaking out, with spurtive quickness, from a long line of bluey figures in front; and, simultaneously, there broke upon our ears an ap-palling crash of sound, the series of fusillades following one another with startling suddenness, which suggested to my somewhat moidered sense a mountain upheaved, with huge rocks tumbling and thundering down a slope, and the echoes rumbling and receding through space. Again and again, these loud and quick explosions were repeated, seemingly with increased violence, until they rose to the highest pitch of fury, and in unbroken continuity. All the world seemed involved in one tremendous ruin!

...

We continued advancing, step by step, loading and firing as we went. To every forward step, they took a backward move, loading and firing as they slowly withdrew. Twenty thousand muskets were being fired at this stage, but, though accuracy of aim was impossible, owing to our labouring hearts, and the jarring and excitement, many bullets found their destined billets on both sides.

After a steady exchange of musketry, which lasted some time, we heard the order: 'Fix Bayonets! On the double-quick!' in tones that thrilled us. There was a simultaneous bound forward, each soul doing his best for the emergency. The Federals appeared inclined to await us; but, at this juncture, our men raised a yell, thousands responded to it, and burst out into the wildest yelling it has ever been my lot to hear. It drove all sanity and order from among us. It served the double purpose of relieving pent-up feelings, and transmitting encouragement along the attacking line. I rejoiced in the shouting like the rest. It reminded me that there were about four hundred companies like the Dixie Greys, who shared our feelings. Most of us, engrossed with the musket-work, had forgotten the fact; but the wave after wave of human voices, louder than all other battle-sounds together, penetrated to every sense, and stimulated our energies to the utmost.

'They fly!' was echoed from lip to lip. It accelerated our pace, and filled us with a noble rage. Then I knew what the Berserker passion was! It deluged us with rapture, and transfigured each Southerner into an exulting victor. At such a moment, nothing could have halted us.

Those savage yells, and the sight of thousands of racing figures coming towards them, discomfited the blue-coats; and when we arrived upon the place where they had stood, they had vanished. Then we caught sight of their beautiful array of tents, before which they had made their stand, after being roused from their Sunday-morning sleep, and huddled into line, at hearing their pickets challenge our skirmishers. The half-dressed dead and wounded showed what a surprise our attack had been. We drew up in the enemy's camp, panting and breathing hard. Some precious minutes were thus lost in recovering our breaths, indulging our curiosity, and re-forming our line. Signs of a hasty rouse to the battle were abundant. Military equipments, uniform-coats, half-packed knapsacks, bedding, of a new and superior quality, littered the company streets.

...

Continuing our advance, we came in view of the tops of another mass of white tents, and, almost at the same time, were met by a furious storm of bullets, poured on us from a long line of blue-coats, whose attitude of assurance proved to us that we should have tough work here. But we were so much heartened by our first success that it would have required a good deal to have halted our advance for long. Their opportunity for making a full impression on us came with terrific suddenness. The world seemed bursting into fragments. Cannon and musket, shell and bullet, lent their several intensities to the distracting uproar. If I had not a fraction of an ear, and an eye inclined towards my Captain and Company, I had been spell-bound by the energies now opposed to us. I likened the cannon, with their deep bass, to the roaring of a great herd of lions; the ripping, cracking musketry, to the incessant yapping of terriers; the windy whisk of shells, and zipping of minie bullets, to the swoop of eagles, and the buzz of angry wasps. All the opposing armies of Grey and Blue fiercely blazed at each other.

After being exposed for a few seconds to this fearful downpour, we heard the order to 'Lie down, men, and continue your firing!' Before me was a prostrate tree, about fifteen inches in diameter, with a narrow strip of light between it and the ground. Behind this shelter a dozen of us flung ourselves. The security it appeared to offer restored me to my individuality. We could fight, and think, and observe, better than out in the open. But it was a terrible period! How the cannon bellowed, and their shells plunged and bounded, and flew with screeching hisses over us!

...

'It is getting too warm, boys!' cried a soldier, and he uttered a vehement curse upon keeping soldiers hugging the ground until every ounce of courage was chilled. He lifted his head a little too high, and a bullet skimmed over the top of the log and hit him fairly in the centre of his forehead, and he fell heavily on his face. But his thought had been instantaneously general; and the officers, with one voice, ordered the charge; and cries of 'Forward, forward!' raised us, as with a spring, to our feet, and changed the complexion of our feelings. The pulse of action beat feverishly once more; and, though overhead was crowded with peril, we were unable to give it so much attention as when we lay stretched on the ground.

Just as we bent our bodies for the onset, a boy's voice cried out, 'Oh, stop, please stop a bit, I have been hurt, and can't move!' I turned to look, and saw Henry Parker, standing on one leg, and dolefully regarding his smashed foot. In another second, we were striding impetuously towards the enemy, vigorously plying our muskets, stopping only to prime the pan and ram the load down, when, with a spring or two, we would fetch up with the front, aim, and fire.

...

It was all very encouraging, for the yelling and shouting were taken up by thousands. "Forward, forward; don't give them breathing time!' was cried. We instinctively obeyed, and soon came in clear view of the blue-coats, who were scornfully unconcerned at first; but, seeing the leaping tide of men coming on at a tremendous pace, their front dissolved, and they fled in double-quick retreat. Again we felt the 'glorious joy of heroes.' It carried us on exultantly, rejoicing in the spirit which recognises nothing but the prey. We were no longer an army of soldiers, but so many school-boys racing, in which length of legs, wind, and condition tell.

We gained the second line of camps, continued the rush through them, and clean beyond. It was now about ten o'clock. My physical powers were quite exhausted, and, to add to my discomfiture, something struck me on my belt-clasp, and tumbled me headlong to the ground.

I could not have been many minutes prostrated before I recovered from the shock of the blow and fall, to find my clasp deeply dented and cracked. My company was not in sight. I was grateful for the rest, and crawled feebly to a tree, and plunging my hand into my haversack, ate ravenously. Within half an hour, feeling renovated, I struck north in the direction which my regiment had taken, over a ground strewn with bodies and the debris of war.

The desperate character of this day's battle was now brought home to my mind in all its awful reality. While in the tumultuous advance, and occupied with a myriad of exciting incidents, it was only at brief intervals that I was conscious of wounds being given and received; but now, in the trail of pursuers and pursued, the ghastly relics appalled every sense. I felt curious as to who the fallen Greys were, and moved to one stretched straight out. It was the body of a stout English Sergeant of a neighbouring company, the members of which hailed principally from the Washita Valley. At the crossing of the Arkansas River this plump, ruddy-faced man had been conspicuous for his complexion, jovial features, and good-humour, and had been nicknamed 'John Bull.' He was now lifeless, and lay with his eyes wide open, regardless of the scorching sun, and the tempestuous cannonade which sounded through the forest, and the musketry that crackled incessantly along the front.

Close by him was a young Lieutenant, who, judging by the new gloss on his uniform, must have been some father's darling. A clean bullet-hole through the centre of his forehead had instantly ended his career. A little further were some twenty bodies, lying in various postures, each by its own pool of viscous blood, which emitted a peculiar scent, which was new to me, but which I have since learned is inseparable from a battle-field. Beyond these, a still larger group lay, body overlying body, knees crooked, arms erect, or wide-stretched and rigid, according as the last spasm overtook them. The company opposed to them must have shot straight.

Other details of that ghastly trail formed a mass of horrors that will always be remembered at the mention of Shiloh. I can never forget the impression those wide-open dead eyes made on me. Each seemed to be starting out of its socket, with a look similar to the fixed wondering gaze of an infant, as though the dying had viewed something appalling at the last moment.

...

An object once seen, if it has affected my imagination, remains indelibly fixed in my memory; and, among many other scenes with which it is now crowded, I cannot forget that half-mile square of woodland, lighted brightly by the sun, and littered by the forms of about a thousand dead and wounded men, and by horses, and military equipments. It formed a picture that may always be reproduced with an almost absolute fidelity. For it was the first Field of Glory I had seen in my May of life, and the first time that Glory sickened me with its repulsive aspect, and made me suspect it was all a glittering lie.

...

I overtook my regiment about one o'clock, and found that it was engaged in one of these occasional spurts of fury. The enemy resolutely maintained their ground, and our side was preparing for another assault. The firing was alternately brisk and slack. We lay down, and availed ourselves of trees, logs, and hollows, and annoyed their upstanding ranks; battery pounded battery, and, meanwhile, we hugged our resting-places closely. Of a sudden, we rose and raced towards the position, and took it by sheer weight and impetuosity, as we had done before. About three o'clock, the battle grew very hot. The enemy appeared to be more concentrated, and immovably sullen. Both sides fired better as they grew more accustomed to the din; but, with assistance from the reserves, we were continually pressing them towards the river Tennessee, without ever retreating an inch.

About this time, the enemy were assisted by the gun-boats, which hurled their enormous projectiles far beyond us; but, though they made great havoc among the trees, and created terror, they did comparatively little damage to those in close touch with the enemy.

...

Finally, about five o'clock, we assaulted and captured a large camp; after driving the enemy well away from it, the front line was as thin as that of a skirmishing body, and we were ordered to retire to the tents. There we hungrily sought after provisions, and I was lucky in finding a supply of biscuits and a canteen of excellent molasses, which gave great comfort to myself and friends. The plunder in the camp was abundant.

...

At daylight, I fell in with my Company ... In a short time, we met our opponents in the same formation as ourselves, and advancing most resolutely. We threw ourselves behind such trees as were near us, fired, loaded, and darted forward to another shelter. Presently, I found myself in an open, grassy space, with no convenient tree or stump near; but, seeing a shallow hollow some twenty paces ahead, I made a dash for it, and plied my musket with haste. I became so absorbed with some blue figures in front of me, that I did not pay sufficient heed to my companion greys; the open space was too danger-ous, perhaps, for their advance; for, had they emerged, I should have known they were pressing forward. Seeing my blues in about the same proportion, I assumed that the greys were keeping their position, and never once thought of re-treat. However, as, despite our firing, the blues were coming uncomfortably near, I rose from my hollow; but, to my speechless amazement, I found myself a solitary grey, in a line of blue skirmishers! My companions had retreated! The next I heard was, 'Down with that gun, Secesh, or I'll drill a hole through you! Drop it, quick!'

Half a dozen of the enemy were covering me at the same instant, and I dropped my weapon, incontinently. Two men sprang at my collar, and marched me, unresisting, into the ranks of the terrible Yankees. I was a prisoner!

When the senses have been concentrated upon a specific object with the intensity which a battle compels, and are forcibly and suddenly veered about by another will, the immediate result is, at first, stupefying. Before my consciousness had returned to me, I was being propelled vigorously from behind, and I was in view of a long, swaying line of soldiers, who were marching to meet us with all the' precision of drill, and with such a close front that a rabbit would have found it difficult to break through. This sight restored me to all my faculties, and I remembered I was a Confederate, in misfortune, and that it behoved me to have some regard for my Uniform. I heard bursts of vituperation from several hoarse throats, which straightened my back and made me defiant.

'Where are you taking that fellow to? Drive a bayonet into the — —! Let him drop where he is!' they cried by the dozen, with a German accent. They grew more excited as we drew nearer, and more men joined in the opprobrious chorus. Then a few dashed from the ranks, with levelled bayonets, to execute what appeared to be the general wish.

I looked into their faces, deformed with fear and fury, and I felt intolerable loathing for the wild-eyed brutes! Their eyes, projected and distended, appeared like spots of pale blue ink, in faces of dough! Reason had fled altogether from their features, and, to appeal for mercy to such blind, ferocious animalism would have been the height of absurdity, but I was absolutely indifferent as to what they might do with me now. Could I have multiplied myself into a thousand, such unintellectual-looking louts might have been brushed out of existence with ease — despite their numbers. They were apparently new troops, from such back-lands as were favoured by German immigrants; and, though of sturdy build, another such mass of savagery and stupidity could not have been found within the four corners of North America. How I wished I could return to the Confederates, and tell them what kind of people were opposing them!

Before their bayonets reached me, my two guards, who were ruddy-faced Ohioans, flung themselves before me, and, presenting their rifles, cried, 'Here! stop that, you fellows! He is our prisoner!' A couple of officers were almost as quick as they, and flourished their swords; and, amid an expenditure of profanity, drove them quickly back into their ranks, cursing and blackguarding me in a manner truly American. A company opened its lines as we passed to the rear. Once through, I was comparatively safe from the Union troops, but not from the Confederate missiles, which were dropping about, and striking men, right and left.

Quickening our pace, we soon were beyond danger from my friends; after which, I looked about with interest at the forces that were marching to retrieve their shame of yesterday. The troops we saw belonged to Buell, who had crossed the Tennessee, and was now joined by Grant. They presented a brave, even imposing, sight; and, in their new uniforms, with glossy knapsacks, rubbers undimmed, brasses resplendent, they approached nearer to my idea of soldiers than our dingy grey troops. Much of this fine show and seeming steadiness was due to their newer equipments, and, as yet, unshaken nerves; but, though their movements were firm, they were languid, and lacked the élan, the bold confidence, of the Southerners. Given twenty-four hours' rest, and the enjoyment of cooked rations, I felt that the Confederates would have crumpled up the handsome Unionists within a brief time.

...

I was a prisoner! Shameful position! What would become of my knapsack, and my little treasures, — letters, and souvenirs of my father? They were lost beyond recovery!

After Stanley's capture, the Union recovery continued; and by the end of the day the Confederates would fall back and accept defeat at the Battle of Shiloh.

The battle served as a wakeup call for both sides, when the dust had settled there were nearly 24,000 casualties suffered between the two armies. This clearly demonstrated the harsh realities and high costs of war. Finally, people on both sides began to realize that this war was not going to be short and glorious; it was going to be long and bloody.

Luckily, Stanley had escaped Shiloh with his life; but little did he know what was waiting for him next...

The Fate of a Prisoner of War

After being captured at Shiloh, Stanley was shipped to the prison at Camp Douglas in Chicago, Illinois. This is his description of what life was like as a prisoner of war...

In our treatment, I think there was a purpose. If so, it may have been from a belief that we should the sooner recover our senses by experiencing as much misery, pain, privation, and sorrow as could be contained within a prison; and, therefore, the authorities rigidly excluded every medical, pious, musical, or literary charity that might have alleviated our sufferings. It was a barbarous age, it is true; but there were sufficient Christian families in Chicago, who, I am convinced, only needed a suggestion, to have formed societies for the relief of the prisoners. And what an opportunity there was for such, to strengthen piety, to promote cheerfulness, soothe political ferocity, and subdue the brutal and vicious passions which possessed those thousands of unhappy youths immured within the horrible pen!

Left to ourselves, with absolutely nothing to do but to brood over our positions, bewail our lots, catch the taint of disease from each other, and passively abide in our prison-pen, we were soon in a fair state of rotting, while yet alive. The reaction from the excitement of the battle-field, and the cheerful presence of exulting thousands, was suspended for a few days by travel up the Mississippi, the generosity of lady-sympathisers in St. Louis, and the trip across Illinois; but, after a few days, it set in strong upon us, when once within the bleak camp at Chicago. Everything we saw and touched added its pernicious influence — the melancholy faces of those who were already wearied with their confinement, the numbers of the sick, the premature agedness of the emaciated, the distressing degeneration of manhood, the plaints of suffering wretches, the increasing bodily discomfort from ever-multiplying vermin, which infested every square inch.

Within a week, our new draft commenced to succumb under the maleficent influences of our surroundings. Our buildings swarmed with vermin, the dust-sweepings were alive with them. The men began to suffer from bilious disorders; dysentery and typhus began to rage. Day after day my company steadily diminished; and every morning I had to see them carried in their blankets to the hospital, whence none ever returned. Those not yet delirious, or too weak to move unaided, we kept with us; but the dysentery — however they contracted it — was of a peculiarly epidemical character, and its victims were perpetually passing us, trembling with weakness, or writhing with pain, exasperating our senses to such a degree that only the strong-minded could forego some expression of their disgust.

The latrines were all at the rear of our plank barracks, and each time imperious nature compelled us to resort to them, we lost a little of that respect and consideration we owed our fellow-creatures. For, on the way thither, we saw crowds of sick men, who had fallen, prostrate from weakness, and given themselves wholly to despair; and, while they crawled or wallowed in their filth, they cursed and blasphemed as often as they groaned. In the edge of the gaping ditches, which provoked the gorge to look at, there were many of the sick people, who, unable to leave, rested there for hours, and made their condition hopeless by breathing the stenchful atmosphere. Exhumed corpses could not have presented anything more hideous than dozens of these dead-and-alive men, who, oblivious to the weather, hung over the latrines, or lay extended along the open sewer, with only a few gasps intervening between them and death. Such as were not too far gone prayed for death, saying, 'Good God, let me die! Let me go, O Lord!' and one insanely damned his vitals and his constitution, because his agonies were so protracted. No self-respecting being could return from their vicinity with-out feeling bewildered by the infinite suffering, his existence degraded, and religion and sentiment blasted.

Yet, indoors, what did we see? Over two hundred un-washed, unkempt, uncombed men, in the dismalest attitudes, occupied in relieving themselves from hosts of vermin, or sunk in gloomy introspection, staring blankly, with heads be-tween their knees, at nothing; weighed down by a surfeit of misery, internal pains furrowing their faces, breathing in a fine cloud of human scurf, and dust of offensive hay, dead to everything but the flitting fancies of the hopeless!

One intelligent and humane supervisor would have wrought wonders at this period with us, and arrested that swift demoralization with which we were threatened. None of us were conspicuously wise out of our own sphere; and of san-itary laws we were all probably as ignorant as of the etiology of sclerosis of the nerve-centres. In our colossal ignorance, we were perhaps doing something half-a-dozen times a day, as dangerous as eating poison, and constantly swallowing a few of the bacilli of typhus. Even had we possessed the necessary science at our finger-tips, we could not have done much, un-aided by the authorities; but when the authorities were as ig-norant as ourselves, — I cannot believe their neglect of us was intentional, — we were simply doomed!

Every morning, the wagons came to the hospital and dead-house, to take away the bodies; and I saw the corpses rolled in their blankets, taken to the vehicles, and piled one upon an-other, as the New Zealand frozen-mutton carcases are carted from the docks!

The statistics of Andersonville are believed to show that the South was even more callous towards their prisoners than the authorities of Camp Douglas were. I admit that we were better fed than the Union prisoners were, and against Colonel Milligan and Mr. Shipman I have not a single accusation to make. It was the age that was brutally senseless, and heedlessly cruel, It was lavish and wasteful of life, and had not the least idea of what civilised warfare ought to be, except in strategy. It was at the end of the flintlock age, a stupid and heartless age, which believed that the application of every variety of torture was better for discipline than kindness, and was guilty, during the war, of enormities that would tax the most saintly to forgive.

Just as the thirties were stupider and crueller than the fifties, and the fifties were more bloody than the seventies, in the mercantile marine service, so a war in the nineties will be much more civilized than the Civil War of the sixties. Those who have survived that war, and have seen brotherly love reestablished, and reconciliation completed, when they think of Andersonville, Libby, Camp Douglas, and other prisons, and of the blood shed in 2,261 battles and skirmishes, must in this present peaceful year needs think that a moral epidemic raged, to have made them so intensely hate then what they profess to love now. Though a democratic government like the American will always be more despotic and arbitrary than that of a constitutional monarchy, even its army will have its Red Cross societies, and Prisoners' Aid Society; and the sights we saw at Camp Douglas will never be seen in America again.

...

The only official connected with Camp Douglas whom I remember with pleasure is Mr. Shipman, the commissary. He was gentlemanly and white-haired, which, added to his unvarying benevolence and politeness, caused him to be regarded by me as something of an agreeable wonder in that pestful yard. After some two days' acquaintance, while drawing the rations, he sounded me as to my intentions. I scarcely comprehended him at the outset, for Camp Douglas was not a place to foster intentions. He explained that, if I were tired of being a prisoner, I could be released by enrolling myself as a Unionist, that is, becoming a Union soldier. My eyes opened very wide at this, and I shook my head, and said, 'Oh, no, I could not do that.' Nothing could have been more unlikely; I had not even dreamed that such an act was possible.

A few days later, I said to Mr. Shipman, 'They have taken two wagon-loads of dead men away this morning.' He gave a sympathetic shrug, as if to say, 'It was all very sad, but what can we do?' He then held forth upon the superiority of the North, the certainty of defeat for the South, the pity it was to see young men throw their lives away for such a cause as slavery, and so on; in short, all that a genuinely kind man, but fervidly Northern, could say. His love embraced Northerners and Southerners alike, for he saw no distinction between them, except that the younger brother had risen to smite the elder, and must be punished until he repented.

But it was useless to try and influence me by political reasons. In the first place, I was too ignorant in politics, and too slow of comprehension, to follow his reasonings; in the second place, every American friend of mine was a Southerner, and my adopted father was a Southerner, and I was blind through my gratitude;

...

But, in the course of six weeks, more powerful influences than Mr. Shipman's gentle reasoning were undermining my resolve to remain as a prisoner. These were the increase in sickness, the horrors of the prison, the oily atmosphere, the ignominious cartage of the dead, the useless flight of time, the fear of being incarcerated for years, which so affected my spirits that I felt a few more days of these scenes would drive me mad. Finally, I was persuaded to accept with several other prisoners the terms of release, and enrolled myself in the U. S. Artillery Service, and, on the 4th June, was once more free to inhale the fresh air.

He had escaped the prison, but he had not escaped the ill-effects of imprisonment. By June 22 his regiment had left him behind at a hospital in Harper's Ferry, West Virginia. He was suffering from the same ailments that had wreaked havoc among his fellow prisoners at Camp Douglas, fever and dysentery.

It was expected that he would rejoin his regiment as soon as he was well enough to follow, but Stanley had different ideas. He decided he didn't really want to fight in the Union Army. So, instead of rejoining his regiment, he deserted, made his way to Baltimore, and sailed to England to visit his family.

By late 1863, he was back in New York working for an alcoholic lawyer whom Stanley referred to as a "Judge" in this brief journal entry: "Boarding with Judge X——. Judge drunk; tried to kill his wife with hatchet; attempted three times. — I held him down all night. Next morning, exhausted; lighted cigar in parlour; wife came down — insulted and raved at me for smoking in her house!"

Moving on from there, Stanley decided to join the Union Navy in August of 1864. In doing so, he become one of only a few men (if not the only one) to serve in both the Confederate and Union Armies, as well as the Union Navy.

He did not stay in the Navy for long, however. In February 1865, Stanley forged passes for himself and a friend. Together, they deserted their ship, the USS Minnesota, and Stanley's involvement in the Civil War was over.

CHAPTER TWO

PAIN, DEATH, WOUNDS, GLORY — THAT WAS THE
SUM OF IT

— THE BATTLE OF HAMPTON ROADS —

On March 8-9, 1862, the Age of Sail was ended, once and for all. While at the same time, the wooden warship became obsolete and was consigned to the pages of history.

March 8th. saw the Confederate ironclad, CSS Virginia, steam into Hampton Roads. There it laid waste to the Union blockade. The USS Cumberland and USS Congress were destroyed, while other ships ran aground or fled for their lives.

That evening, the Union ironclad, USS Monitor, arrived on the scene; and the next day there was a fight for the ages. For the first time in history, two ironclad warships met in battle. When the smoke had cleared, it was obvious that iron and steam were the future of naval warfare.

Following are two accounts[2] of the Battle of Hampton Roads. One account is from the Chief Engineer of the Virginia, and the other is from the two men who commanded the Monitor.

These accounts are a great illustration of how different two accounts of the same event can be.

---

[2] Taken from *The Monitor and The Merrimac Both Sides of The Story*, by J.L. Worden, S.D. Greene, and H. Ashton Ramsay, 1912.

The View from the CSS Virginia (Merrimac)

H. Ashton Ramsay was involved in the conversion of the old, wooden USS Merrimac into the ironclad CSS Virginia, and he was the Chief Engineer aboard the Virginia during the Battle of Hampton Roads. Here he describes his experiences aboard the Virginia in the days leading up to and during the Battle of Hampton Roads...

Even naval officers were skeptical as to the result.

...

I remember that my old friend and comrade, Captain Charles MacIntosh, while awaiting orders, used to come over and stand on the granite curbing of the dock to watch the work as it crawled along.

"Good-by, Ramsay," he said, sadly, on the eve of starting to command a ram at New Orleans. "I shall never see you again. She will prove your coffin." A short time afterward the poor fellow had both legs shot from under him and died almost immediately.

...

Many details remained uncompleted when we were at last floated out of dry-dock, but there was great pressure for us to make some demonstration that might serve to check McClellan in his advance up the Peninsula.

The ship was still full of workmen hurrying her to completion when Commodore Franklin Buchanan arrived from Richmond one March morning and ordered everyone out of the ship, except her crew of three hundred and fifty men which had been hastily drilled on shore in the management of the big guns, and directed Executive Officer Jones to prepare to sail at once.

At that time nothing was known of our destination. All we knew was that we were off at last. Buchanan sent for me. The veteran sailor, the beau ideal of a naval officer of the old school, with his tall form, harsh features, and clear, piercing eyes, was pacing the deck with a stride I found it difficult to match, although he was then over sixty and I but twenty-four.

"Ramsay," he asked, "what would happen to your engines and boilers if there should be a collision?"

"They are braced tight," I assured him. "Though the boilers stand fourteen feet, they are so securely fastened that no collision could budge them."

"I am going to ram the Cumberland," said my commander. "I'm told she has the new rifled guns, the only ones in their whole fleet we have cause to fear. The moment we are in the Roads I'm going to make right for her and ram her. How about your engines? They were in bad shape in the old ship, I understand. Can we rely on them? Should they be tested by a trial trip?"

"She will have to travel some ten miles down the river before we get to the Roads," I said. "If any trouble develops I'll report it. I think that will be [a] sufficient trial trip."

...

Across the river at Newport News gleamed the batteries and white tents of the Federal camp and the vessels of the fleet blockading the mouth of the James, chief among them the Congress and the Cumberland, tall and stately, with every line and spar clearly defined against the blue March sky, their decks and ports bristling with guns, while the rigging of the Cumberland was gay with the red, white, and blue of sailors' garments hung out to dry.

As we rounded into view the white-winged sailing craft that sprinkled the bay and long lines of tugs and small boats scurried to the far shore like chickens on the approach of a hovering hawk. They had seen our black hulk which looked like the roof of a barn afloat. Suddenly huge volumes of smoke began to pour from the funnels of the frigates Minnesota and Roanoke at Old Point. They had seen us, too, and were getting up steam. Bright-colored signal flags were run up and down the masts of all the ships of the Federal fleet. The Congress shook out her topsails. Down came the clothes-line on the Cumberland, and boats were lowered and dropped astern.

Our crew was summoned to the gun-deck, and Buchanan addressed us: "Sailors, in a few minutes you will have the long-looked-for opportunity of showing your devotion to our cause. Remember that you are about to strike for your country and your homes. The Confederacy expects every man to do his duty. Beat to quarters." Every terse, burning word is engraved on my memory, though fifty years have passed since they were spoken.

...

Passing along the gun-deck, I saw the pale and determined countenances of the guns' crews, as they stood motionless at their posts, with set lips unsmiling, contrasting with the care-less expression of sailors when practised at "fighting quarters" on a man-of-war. This was the real thing.

As we approached the Federal ships we were met by a veri-table storm of shells which must have sunk any ship then afloat—except the Merrimac. They struck our sloping sides, were deflected upward to burst harmlessly in the air, or rolled down and fell hissing into the water, dashing the spray up into our ports.

As we drew nearer the Cumberland, above the roar of battle rang the voice of Buchanan, "Do you surrender?"

"Never!" retorted the gallant Morris.

The crux of what followed was down in the engine-room. Two gongs, the signal to stop, were quickly followed by three, the signal to reverse. There was an ominous pause, then a crash, shaking us all off our feet. The engines labored. The vessel was shaken in every fiber. Our bow was visibly depressed. We seemed to be bearing down with a weight on our prow. Thud, thud, thud, came the rain of shot on our shield from the double-decked battery of the Congress. There was a terrible crash in the fire-room. For a moment we thought one of the boilers had burst. No, it was the explosion of a shell in our stack. Was any one hit? No, thank God! The firemen had been warned to keep away from the up-take, so the fragments of shell fell harmlessly on the iron floor-plates.

We had rushed on the doomed ship, relentless as fate, crashing through her barricade of heavy spars and torpedo fenders, striking her below her starboard fore-chains, and crushing far into her. For a moment the whole weight of her hung on our prow and threatened to carry us down with her, the return wave of the collision curling up into our bow port.

The Cumberland began to sink slowly, bow first, but continued to fight desperately for the forty minutes that elapsed after her doom was sealed, while we were engaged with both the Cumberland and the Congress, being right between them.

We had left our cast-iron beak in the side of the Cumberland. Like the wasp, we could sting but once, leaving it in the wound.

Battle of Hampton Roads (March 9, 1862).

Our smoke-stack was riddled, our flag was shot down several times, and was finally secured to a rent in the stack. On our gun-deck the men were fighting like demons. There was no thought or time for the wounded and dying as they tugged away at their guns, training and sighting their pieces while the orders rang out, "Sponge, load, fire!"

"The muzzle of our gun has been shot away," cried one of the gunners.

"No matter, keep on loading and firing—do the best you can with it," replied Lieutenant Jones.

...

This gives some faint notion of the scene passing behind our grim iron casement, which to the beholders without seemed a machine of destruction. Human hearts were beating and bleeding there. Human lives were being sacrificed. Pain, death, wounds, glory — that was the sum of it.

On the doomed ship Cumberland the battle raged with equal fury. The sanded deck was red and slippery with blood.

Delirium seized the crew. They stripped to their trousers, kicked off their shoes, tied handkerchiefs about their heads, and fought and cheered as their ship sank beneath their feet. Then the order came, "All save who can." There was a scramble for the spar-deck and a rush overboard. The ship listed. The after pivot-gun broke loose and rushed down the decline like a furious animal, rolling over a man as it bounded overboard, leaving a mass of mangled flesh on deck.

We now turned to the Congress, which had tried to escape but had grounded, and the battle raged once more, broadside upon broadside, delivered at close range, the Merrimac working closer all the time with her bow pointed as if to ram the Congress. A shell from Lieutenant Wood's gun sped through their line of powder-passers, not only cutting down the men, but exploding the powder buckets in their hands, spreading death and destruction and setting fire to the ship.

At last came the order, "Cease firing."

"The Congress has surrendered," someone cried. "Look out of the port. See, she has run up white flags. The officers are waving their handkerchiefs."

At this several of the officers started to leave their posts and rush on deck, but Lieutenant Jones in his stentorian voice sang out: "Stand by your guns, and, lieutenants, be ready to resume firing at the word. See that your guns are well supplied with ammunition during the lull. Dr. Garnett, see how those poor fellows yonder are coming on. Mr. Littlepage, tell Paymaster Semple to have a care of the berth-deck and use every precaution against fire. Mr. Hasker, call away the cutter's crew and have them in readiness. Mr. Lindsay [to the carpenter], sound the well, examine the forehold, and report if you find anything wrong." Such was Catesby Ap. R. Jones, the executive officer of the Merrimac.

When it was fully evident that there was to be a suspension of hostilities, and these details had all been attended to, several of the officers went to stand beside Buchanan on the upper grating.

The whole scene was changed. A pall of black smoke hung about the ships and obscured the clean-cut outlines of the shore. Down the river were the three frigates St. Lawrence, Roanoke, and Minnesota, also enveloped in the clouds of battle that now and then reflected the crimson lightnings of the god of war. The masts of the Cumberland were protruding above the water. The Congress presented a terrible scene of carnage.

The gunboats Beaufort and Raleigh were signaled to take off the wounded and fire the ship. They were driven away by sharpshooters on shore, who suddenly turned their fire on us, notwithstanding the white flag of the Congress. Buchanan fell, severely wounded in the groin.

As he was being carried below he said to Executive Officer Jones: "Plug hot shot into her and don't leave her until she's afire. They must look after their own wounded, since they won't let us" — a characteristic command when it is remembered that his own brother, McKean Buchanan, was paymaster of the Congress and might have been numbered among the wounded.

We had kept two furnaces for the purpose of heating shot. They were rolled into the flames on a grating, rolled out into iron buckets, hoisted to the gun-deck, and rolled into the guns, which had been prepared with wads of wet hemp. Then the gun would be touched off quickly and the shot sent on its errand of destruction.

Leaving the Congress wrapped in sheets of flame, we made for the three other frigates. The St. Lawrence and Roanoke had run aground, but were pulled off by tugs and made their escape. The Minnesota was not so fortunate, but we drew twenty-three feet of water and could not get near enough to destroy her, while our guns could not be elevated owing to the narrow embrasures, and their range was only a mile; so we made for our moorings at Sewall's Point.

All the evening we stood on deck watching the brilliant display of the burning ship. Every part of her was on fire at the same time, the red-tongued flames running up shrouds, masts, and stays, and extending out to the yard-arms. She stood in bold relief against the black background, lighting up the Roads and reflecting her lurid lights on the bosom of the now placid and hushed waters. Every now and then the flames would reach one of the loaded cannon and a shell would hiss at random through the darkness. About midnight came the grand finale. The magazines exploded, shooting up a huge column of firebrands hundreds of feet in the air, and then the burning hulk burst asunder and melted into the waters, while the calm night spread her sable mantle over Hampton Roads.

The Monitor arrived during the evening and anchored under the stern of the Minnesota, her lighter draught enabling her to do so without danger. To us the ensuing engagement was in the nature of a surprise. If we had known we were to meet her we would have at least been supplied with solid shot for our rifled guns. We might even have thought best to wait until our iron beak, lost in the side of the Cumberland, could be replaced. Buchanan was incapacitated by his wound, and the command devolved upon Lieutenant Jones.

We left our anchorage shortly before eight o'clock next morning and steamed across and up stream toward the Minnesota, thinking to make short work of her and soon return with her colors trailing under ours. We approached her slowly, feeling our way cautiously along the edge of the channel, when suddenly, to our astonishment, a black object that looked like the historic description, "a barrel-head afloat with a cheese-box on top of it," moved slowly out from under the Minnesota and boldly confronted us. It must be confessed that both ships were queer-looking craft, as grotesque to the eyes of the men of '62 as they would appear to those of the present generation.

And now the great fight was on, a fight the like of which the world had never seen. With the battle of yesterday old methods had passed away, and with them the experience of a thousand years "of battle and of breeze" was brought to naught.

We hovered about each other in spirals, gradually contracting the circuits until we were within point-blank range, but our shell glanced from the Monitor's turret just as hers did from our sloping sides. For two hours the cannonade continued without perceptible damage to either of the combatants.

On our gun-deck all was bustle, smoke, grimy figures, and stern commands, while down in the engine and boiler rooms the sixteen furnaces were belching out fire and smoke, and the firemen standing in front of them, like so many gladiators, tugged away with devil's-claw and slice-bar, inducing by their exertions more and more intense combustion and heat. The noise of the cracking, roaring fires, escaping steam, and the loud and labored pulsations of the engines, together with the roar of battle above and the thud and vibration of the huge masses of iron which were hurled against us produced a scene and sound to be compared only with the poet's picture of the lower regions.

And then an accident occurred that threatened our utter destruction. We stuck fast aground on a sand-bar.

Our situation was critical. The Monitor could, at her leisure, come close up to us and yet be out of our reach, owing to our inability to deflect our guns. In she came and began to sound every chink in our armor—everyone but that which was actually vulnerable, had she known it.

The coal consumption of the two days' fight had lightened our prow until our unprotected submerged deck was almost awash. The armor on our sides below the water-line had been extended but about three feet, owing to our hasty departure before the work was finished. Lightened as we were, these exposed portions rendered us no longer an ironclad, and the Monitor might have pierced us between wind and water had she depressed her guns.

Fearing that she might discover our vulnerable "heel of Achilles" we had to take all chances. We lashed down the safety valves, heaped quick-burning combustibles into the already raging fires, and brought the boilers to a pressure that would have been unsafe under ordinary circumstances. The propeller churned the mud and water furiously, but the ship did not stir. We piled on oiled cotton waste, splints of wood, anything that would burn faster than coal. It seemed impossible that the boilers could stand the pressure we were crowding upon them. Just as we were beginning to despair there was a perceptible movement, and the Merrimac slowly dragged herself off the shoal by main strength. We were saved.

Before our adversary saw that we were again afloat we made a dash for her, catching her quite unprepared, and tried to ram her, but our commander was dubious about the result of a collision without our iron-shod beak, and gave the signal to reverse the engines long before we reached the Monitor. As a result I did not feel the slightest shock down in the engine-room, though we struck her fairly enough.

The carpenter reported that the effect was to spring a leak forward. Lieutenant Jones sent for me and asked me about it.

"It is impossible we can be making much water," I replied, "for the skin of the vessel is plainly visible in the crank-pits."

A second time he sent for me and asked if we were making any water in the engine-room.

"With the two large Worthington pumps, besides the bilge injections, we could keep her afloat for hours, even with a ten-inch shell in her hull," I assured him, repeating that there was no water in the engine and boiler rooms.

We glided past, leaving the Monitor unscathed, but got between her and the Minnesota and opened fire on the latter. The Monitor gallantly rushed to her rescue, passing so close under our submerged stern that she almost snapped off our propeller. As she was passing, so near that we could have leaped aboard her, Lieutenant Wood trained the stern-gun on her when she was only twenty yards from its muzzle and delivered a rifle-pointed shell which dislodged the iron logs sheltering the Monitor's conning-tower, carrying away the steering-gear and signal apparatus, and blinding Captain Worden. It was a mistake to place the conning-tower so far from the turret and the vitals of the ship. Since that time it has been located over the turret. The Monitor's turret was a death-trap. It was only twenty feet in diameter, and every shot knocked off bolt-heads and sent them flying against the gunners. If one of them barely touched the side of the turret he would be stunned and momentarily paralyzed. Lieutenant Greene had been taken below in a dazed condition and never fully recovered from the effects. One of the port shutters had been jammed, putting a gun out of commission, and there was nothing for the Monitor to do but to retreat and leave the Minnesota to her fate.

Captain Van Brunt, of the latter vessel, thought he was now doomed and was preparing to fire his ship when he saw the Merrimac also withdrawing toward Norfolk.

It was at this juncture that Lieutenant Jones had sent for me and said: "The pilots will not place us nearer to the Minnesota, and we cannot afford to run the risk of getting aground again. I'm going to haul off under the guns of Sewall's Point and renew the attack on the rise of the tide. Bank your fires and make any necessary adjustments to the machinery, but be prepared to start up again later in the afternoon."

I went below to comply with his instructions, and later was astonished to hear cheering. Rushing on deck, I found we were passing Craney Island on our way to Norfolk, and were being cheered by the soldiers of the battery.

Our captain had consulted with some of his lieutenants. He explained afterward that as the Monitor had proved herself so formidable an adversary he had thought best to get a supply of solid shot, have the prow replaced, the port shutters put on, the armor belt extended below water, and the guns whose muzzles had been shot away replaced, and then renew the engagement with every chance of victory. I remember feeling as though a wet blanket had been thrown over me. His reasoning was doubtless good, but it ignored the moral effect of leaving the Roads without forcing the Minnesota to surrender.

As the Merrimac passed up the river, trailing the ensign of the Congress under the stars and bars, she received a tremendous ovation from the crowds that lined the shores, while hundreds of small boats, gay with flags and bunting, converted our course into a triumphal procession.

The View from the USS Monitor

Obviously the Confederates felt they had won the battle; but as we will see, the Union sailors felt the same way. The following account is from the commander of the USS Monitor Lieutenant John L. Worden, up until the point in the battle when he was wounded. Interestingly, Lieutenant Worden addresses the bolt heads in the Monitor's turret, but his account contradicts what H. Ashton Ramsay had to say about them.

...we left New York Harbor in some haste. We had information that the Merrimac was nearly completed, and if we were to fight her on her first appearance, we must be on the ground. The Monitor had been hurried from the laying of her keel. Her engines were new, and her machinery did not move smoothly. Never was a vessel launched that so much needed trial-trips to test her machinery and get her crew accustomed to their novel duties. We went to sea practically without them. No part of the vessel was finished; there was one omission that was serious, and came very near causing her failure and the loss of many lives. In heavy weather it was intended that her hatches and all her openings should be closed and battened down. In that case all the men would be below, and would have to depend upon artificial ventilation. Our machinery for that purpose proved wholly inadequate.

We were in a heavy gale of wind as soon as we passed Sandy Hook. The vessel behaved splendidly. The seas rolled over her, and we found her the most comfortable vessel we had ever seen, except for the ventilation, which gave us more trouble than I have time to tell you about. We had to run into port and anchor on account of the weather, and, as you know, it was two o'clock in the morning of Sunday before we were alongside the Minnesota. Captain Van Brunt gave us an account of Saturday's experience. He was very glad to make our acquaintance, and notified us that we must be prepared to receive the Merrimac at daylight. We had had a very hard trip down the coast, and officers and men were weary and sleepy. But when informed that our fight would probably open at daylight, and that the Monitor must be put in order, every man went to his post with a cheer. That night there was no sleep on board the Monitor.

In the gray of the early morning we saw a vessel approaching, which our friends on the Minnesota said was the Merrimac. Our fastenings were cast off, our machinery started, and we moved out to meet her half-way. We had come a long way to fight her, and did not intend to lose our opportunity.

...there were three possible points of weakness in the Monitor, two of which might have been guarded against in her construction, if there had been more time to perfect her plans. One of them was in the turret, which, as you see, is constructed of eight plates of inch iron—on the side of the ports, nine—set on end so as to break joints, and firmly bolted together, making a hollow cylinder eight inches thick. It rests on a metal ring on a vertical shaft, which is revolved by power from the boilers. If a projectile struck the turret at an acute angle, it was expected to glance off without doing damage. But what would happen if it was fired in a straight line to the center of the turret, which in that case would receive the whole force of the blow? It might break off the bolt-heads on the interior, which, flying across, would kill the men at the guns; it might disarrange the revolving mechanism, and then we would be wholly disabled.

I laid the Monitor close alongside the Merrimac, and gave her a shot. She returned our compliment by a shell weighing one hundred and fifty pounds, fired when we were close together, which struck the turret so squarely that it received the whole force. Here you see the scar, two and a half inches deep in the wrought iron, a perfect mold of the shell. If anything could test the turret, it was that shot. It did not start a rivethead or a nut! It stunned the two men who were nearest where the ball struck, and that was all. I touched the lever—the turret revolved as smoothly as before.

...

I had decided how I would fight her in advance. I would keep the Monitor moving in a circle just large enough to give time for loading the guns. At the point where the circle impinged upon the Merrimac our guns should be fired, and loaded while we were moving around the circuit. Evidently the Merrimac would return the compliment every time. At our second exchange of shots, she returning six or eight to our two, another of her large shells struck our 'plank-shear' at its angle, and tore up one of the deck-plates, as you see. The shell had struck what I believed to be the weakest point in the Monitor. We had already learned that the Merrimac swarmed with sharpshooters, for their bullets were constantly spattering against our turret and our deck. If a man showed himself on deck he would draw their fire. But I did not much consider the sharpshooters. It was my duty to investigate the effects of that shot. I ordered one of the pendulums to be hauled aside, and, crawling out of the port, walked to the side, lay down upon my chest, and examined it thoroughly. The hull was un-injured, except for a few splinters in the wood. I walked back and crawled into the turret—the bullets were falling on the iron deck all about me as thick as hail-stones in a storm. None struck me, I suppose because the vessel was moving, and at the angle, and when I was lying on the deck my body made a small mark, difficult to hit. We gave them two more guns, and then I told the men, what was true, that the Merrimac could not sink us if we let her pound us for a month. The men cheered; the knowledge put new life into all.

We had more exchanges, and then the Merrimac tried new tactics. She endeavored to ram us, to run us down. Once she struck us about amidships with her iron ram. Here you see its mark. It gave us a shock, pushed us around, and that was all the harm. But the movement placed our sides together. I gave her two guns, which I think lodged in her side, for, from my lookout crack, I could not see that either shot rebounded. Ours being the smaller vessel, and more easily handled, I had no difficulty in avoiding her ram. I ran around her several times, planting our shot in what seemed to be the most vulnerable places. In this way, reserving my fire until I got the range and the mark, I planted two more shots almost in the very spot I had hit when she tried to ram us. Those shots must have been effective, for they were followed by a shower of bars of iron.

The third weak spot was our pilot-house. You see that it is built a little more than three feet above the deck, of bars of iron, ten by twelve inches square, built up like a log-house, bolted with very large bolts at the corners where the bars interlock. The pilot stands upon a platform below, his head and shoulders in the pilot-house. The upper tier of bars is separated from the second by an open space of an inch, through which the pilot may look out at every point of the compass. The pilot-house, as you see, is a foursquare mass of iron, provided with no means of deflecting a ball. I expected trouble from it, and I was not disappointed. Until my accident happened, as we approached the enemy I stood in the pilot-house and gave the signals. Lieutenant Greene fired the guns, and Engineer Stimers, here, revolved the turret.

I was below the deck when the corner of the pilot-house was first struck by a shot or a shell. It either burst or was broken, and no harm was done. A short time after I had given the signal and, with my eye close against the lookout crack, was watching the effect of our shot, something happened to me — my part in the fight was ended. Lieutenant Greene, who fought the Merrimac until she had no longer stomach for fighting, will tell you the rest of the story.

...

Here Lieutenant Greene takes over the story and tells what happened after he took over command of the Monitor.

I cannot add much to the Captain's story, he had cut out the work for us, and we had only to follow his pattern. I kept the Monitor either moving around the circle or around the enemy, and endeavored to place our shots as near her amidships as possible, where Captain Worden believed he had already broken through her armor. We knew that she could not sink us, and I thought I would keep right on pounding her as long as she would stand it. There is really nothing new to be added to Captain Worden's account. We could strike her wherever we chose. Weary as they must have been, our men were full of enthusiasm, and I do not think we wasted a shot. Once we ran out of the circle for a moment to adjust a piece of machinery, and I learn that some of our friends feared that we were drawing out of the fight. The Merrimac took the opportunity to start for Norfolk. As soon as our machinery was adjusted we followed her, and got near enough to give her a parting shot. But I was not familiar with the locality; there might be torpedoes planted in the channel, and I did not wish to take any risk of losing our vessel, so I came back to the company of our friends.

...

The reporter who recorded the accounts of Lieutenants Worden and Greene also had this to say about the pilot house where Lieutenant Worden was injured.

We were then shown the injury to the pilot-house. The mark of the ball was plain upon the two upper bars, the principal impact being upon the lower of the two. This huge bar was broken in the middle, but held firmly at either end. The farther it was pressed in, the stronger was the resistance on the exterior. On the inside the fracture in the bar was half an inch wide. Captain Worden's eye was very near to the lookout crack, so that when the gun was discharged the shock of the ball knocked him senseless, while the mass of flame filled one side of his face with coarse grains of powder. He remained insensible for some hours.

CHAPTER THREE

THE DESIGN WAS HAZARDOUS IN THE EXTREME

— CLANDESTINE ACTIVITY —

*D*uring the Civil War, there was quite a bit that went on in the shadows: Confederate raids from Canada, prison escapes, slave escapes, secret agents, and undercover spies. The list could go on and on. The Civil War heroes with the most exciting stories are often the ones we know the least about. Names like Belle Boyd, Lafayette Baker, Sam Davis, Mary Bowser, Rose O'Neal Greenhow, and Timothy Webster should be better known.

Without a doubt, the things these people went through in service to their countries were amazing. Sometimes they even put James Bond to shame.

In this chapter you will be introduced to the stories of three people who pulled off some pretty cool stuff right under the noses of their enemies...

Robert Smalls

First up is the story of Robert Smalls. Without a doubt, one of the most amazing stories I have ever heard.

Robert was a slave in Charleston, South Carolina, when he (along with his family and some other slaves) took the Confederate steamship Planter, sailed her out of the harbor under all the Confed-

erate guns (giving all the correct signals as they went), and escaped to the Union blockading squadron outside the harbor.

Not only that, but he went on to serve first as pilot, later as a Captain aboard the Planter in service to the Union Army. Furthermore, after the war he served in the U.S Congress as a Representative from South Carolina.

Unfortunately, I could not find an account of this daring escape written by Robert Smalls, so I have pieced together what I could find. In the following letter[3] he states that he is in the service of the Navy, and he mentions his escape...

Robt. Smalls, the negro pilot who brought the Rebel steamer Planter out of Charleston, and delivered her to our naval forces, publishes the following letter in the Washington Republican:

Mr. Editor: In your paper of yesterday it is stated that an application had been made by me to Senator Pomeroy for a passage to Central America. I wish it understood that I have made no such application; but, at the same time, I would express my cordial approval of every kind and wise effort for the liberation and elevation of my oppressed race.

After waiting, apparently in vain, for many years for our deliverance, a party consisting of nine men, myself included, of the City of Charleston, conferred freedom on ourselves, five women and three children; and to the Government of the United States we gave the Planter, a gunboat which cost nearly $30,000, together with six large guns, from a 24-pounder howitzer to a 100-pound Parrot rifle.

We are all now in the service of the navy, under the command of our true friend, Rear Admiral Dupont, where we

---

[3] Taken from the *Belmont Chronicle (St. Clairsville, Ohio)*, September 11, 1862.

wish to serve till the Rebellion and Slavery are alike crushed out for ever.

Very respectfully,
Robert Smalls,
Washington, D.C. August 27, 1862

Robert Smalls after he captured the *Planter*.

Following is a report[4] on the exploits of Robert Smalls during the war. It was filed by the Committee on Naval Affairs during the second session of the 47th Congress of the United States. In this report, the Committee reports not only on his escape, but also on his heroic

---

[4] Taken from *Reports of Committees of the House of Representatives for the Second Session of the Forty-Ninth Congress*, 1887.

service throughout the war. Note: the report misidentifies the Plant-er's captain as "Captain Relay," his name was Captain C.J. Relyea.

The facts on which this claim is based were investigated by the Committee on Naval Affairs of the Forty-seventh Congress, and were as follows, as embodied in the report of that committee:

On May 13, 1862, the Confederate steamboat Planter, the special dispatch-boat of General Ripley, the Confederate post commander at Charleston, S. C, was taken, by Robert Smalls under the following circumstances from the wharf at which she was lying, carried safely out of Charleston Harbor, and delivered to one of the vessels of the Federal fleet then block-ading that port:

On the day previous, May 12, the Planter, which had for two weeks been engaged in removing guns from Cole's Island to James Island, returned to Charleston. That night all the of-ficers went ashore and slept in the city, leaving on board a crew of eight men, all colored. Among them was Robert Smalls, who was virtually the pilot of the boat, although he was only called a wheelman, because at that time no colored man could have, in fact, been made a pilot. For some time previous he had been watching for an opportunity to carry into execution a plan he had conceived to take the Planter to the Federal fleet. This, he saw, was about as good a chance as he would ever have to do so, and therefore he determined not to lose it. Consulting with the balance of the crew, Smalls found that they were willing to co-operate with him, although two of them afterwards concluded to remain behind. The de-sign was hazardous in the extreme. The boat would have to pass beneath the guns of the forts in the harbor. Failure and detection would have been certain death. Fearful was the venture, but it was made. The daring resolution had been formed, and under command of Robert Smalls wood was taken aboard, steam was put on, and with her valuable cargo of guns and ammunition, intended for Fort Ripley, a new fortification just constructed in the harbor, about two o'clock in the morning the Planter silently moved off from her dock, steamed up to North Atlantic wharf, where Smalls's wife and two children, together with four other women and one other child, and also three men, were waiting to embark. All these were taken on board, and then, at 3.25 a. m., May 13, the Planter started on her perilous adventure, carrying nine men, five women, and three children. Passing Fort Johnson, the Planter's steam-whistle blew the usual salute and she proceeded down the bay. Approaching Fort Sumter, Smalls stood in the pilot-house leaning out of the window, with his arms folded across his breast, after the manner of Captain Relay, the commander of the boat, and his head covered with the huge straw hat which Captain Relay commonly wore on such occasions.

The signal required to be given by all steamers passing out was blown as coolly as if General Ripley was on board, going out on a tour of inspection. Sumter answered by signal, "All right," and the Planter headed toward Morris Island, then occupied by Hatch's light artillery, and passed beyond the range of Sumter's guns before anybody suspected anything was wrong. When at last the Planter was obviously going toward the Federal fleet off the bar, Sumter signaled toward Morris Island to stop her. But it was too late. As the Planter approached the Federal fleet, a white flag was displayed, but this was not at first discovered, and the Federal steamers, supposing the Confederate rams were coming to attack them, stood out to deep water. But the ship Onward, Captain Nichols, which was not a steamer, remained, opened her ports, and was about to fire into the Planter, when she noticed the flag of truce. As soon as the vessels came within hailing distance of each other, the Planter's errand was explained. Captain Nichols then boarded her, and Smalls delivered the Planter to him. From the Planter, Smalls was transferred to the Augusta, the flag-ship off the bar, under the command of Captain Parrott, by whom the Planter, with Smalls and her crew, were sent to Port Royal, to Rear-Admiral Du Pont, then in command of the Southern squadron.

Captain Smalls was soon afterwards ordered to Edisto to join the gunboat Crusader, Captain Rhind. He then proceeded in the Crusader, piloting her and followed by the Planter, to Simmous's Bluff, on Wadmalaw Sound, where a sharp battle was fought between these boats and a Confederate light battery and some infantry. The Confederates were driven out of their works, and the troops on the Planter landed and captured all the tents and provisions of the enemy. This occurred sometime in June, 1862.

Captain Smalls continued to act as pilot on board the Planter and the Crusader, and as blockading pilot between Charleston and Beaufort. He made repeated trips up and along the rivers near the coast, pointing out and removing the torpedoes which he himself had assisted in sinking and putting in position. During these trips he was present in several fights at Adams's Run, on the Dawho River, where the Planter was hotly and severely fired upon: also at Rockville, John's Island, and other places. Afterwards he was ordered back to Port Royal, whence he piloted the fleet up Broad River to Pocotaligo, where a very severe battle ensued. Captain Smalls was the pilot on the monitor Keokuk, Captain Ryan, in the memorable attack on Fort Sumter, on the afternoon of the 7th of April, 1863. In this attack the Keokuk was struck ninety-six times, nineteen shots passing through her. She retired from the engagement only to sink on the next morning, near Light-House Inlet. Captain Smalls left her just before she went down, and was taken with the remainder of the crew on board of the Ironsides. The next day the fleet returned to Hilton Head.

When General Gillmore took command Smalls became pilot in the quartermaster's department in the expedition on Morris Island. He was then stationed as pilot of the Stono, where he remained until the United States troops took possession of the south end of Morris Island, when he was put in charge of Light House Inlet as pilot.

Upon one occasion, in December, 1863, while the Planter, then under Captain Nickerson, was sailing through Folly Island Creek the Confederate batteries at Secessionville opened a very hot fire upon her. Captain Nickerson became demoralized and left the pilot-house and secured himself in the coal-bunker. Smalls was on the deck, and finding out that the captain had deserted his post, entered the pilot-house, took command of the boat, and carried her safely out of the reach of the guns. For this conduct he was promoted by order of General Gillmore, commanding the Department of the South, to the rank of captain, and was ordered to act as captain of the Planter, which was used as a supply-boat along the coast until the end of the war. In September, 1866, he carried his boat to Baltimore, where she was put out of commission and sold.

Besides the daring enterprise of Captain Smalls in bringing out the Planter, his gallant conduct in rescuing her a second time, for which he was made captain of her, and his invaluable services to the Army and Navy as a pilot in waters where he perfectly knew not only every bank and bar, but also where every torpedo was situated, there are still other elements to be considered in estimating the value of Captain Smalls' services to the country. The Planter on the 13th of May, 1862, was a most useful and important vessel to the enemy. The loss of her was a severe blow to the enemy's service in carrying supplies and troops to different points of the harbor and river fortifications. At the very time of the seizure she had on board the armament for Fort Ripley. The Planter was taken by the Government at a valuation of $9,000, one-half of which was paid to the captain and crew, the captain receiving one-third of one- half, or $1,500. Upon what principle the Government claimed one-half of this capture cannot be divined, nor yet how this disposition could have been made of her without any judicial proceeding. That $9,000 was an absurdly low valuation for the Planter is abundantly shown by facts stated in the affidavits of Charles H. Campbell and E. M. Baldwin, which are appended. In addition thereto their sworn average valuation of the Planter was $67,500. The report of Montgomery Sicard, commander and inspector of ordnance, to Commodore Patterson, navy-yard commandant, shows that the cargo of the Planter, as raw material, was worth $3,043.05; that at ante-bellum prices it was worth $7,163.35, and at war prices $10,290.60. For this cargo the government has never paid one dollar. It is a severe comment on the justice as well as the boasted generosity of the Government that, whilst it had received $60,000 to $70,000 -worth of property at the hands of Captain Smalls, it has paid him the trifling amount of $1,500, and for twenty years his gallant daring and distinguished and valuable services which he has rendered to the country have been wholly unrecognized.

Mr. Smalls was never awarded any further prize money, despite the compelling case presented by the Committee.

Hanged as a Spy

This is an interesting story[5] I came across in my research. It was an interview of the Reverend J. T. Mann, originally published in The Pensacola (Florida) Journal on June 26, 1906. I could not find the name of the reporter who conducted the interview, nor could I find much about Mr. Mann other than this interview. Hopefully I will be able to learn more about this interesting story in the future.

Basically, in this interview, Mr. Mann recounts his service in the Confederate Army as a soldier and a spy. He tells of his capture and attempted hanging, as well as his subsequent rescue at the hands of a Union officer who believed him to be innocent. He includes a colorful account of the "sensations of being hanged" (including an "out of body experience"), and also gives an account of his final escape from Fort Barrancas.

… you ask me to tell you the sensations of being hanged. Well, to be truthful, there are not enough adjectives in the unabridged to describe the sensations. It is so wonderfully painful that a person would have to undergo the experience to realize to the fullest extent all that is felt. But, I will tell you as best I can how I felt when the noose was around my neck, but in order to do so, I will have to detail a little Civil War History, how I came to be a Confederate spy, and my subsequent capture at Fort Barrancas.

---

[5] Taken from *A Spy in the Service of the Confederacy*, 1908.

While quite a young man I enlisted as a private in Company H, Bogart Guards, commanded by Captain George Meyhi, of the Third Louisiana Battalion of "Tigers," which was commanded by Lieut.-Col. L. S. Bradford. I received my baptism of fire at Mechanicsville in July, 1862, in the seven days' fight around Richmond, and at Gaines' Mill, sustained a slight wound in the left hand and a bullet passed through the back of my neck, which nearly uncoupled life and body. In the battle of Manassas I was wounded in the right hip and left thigh, and this was how I came to be a spy. As soon as I was out of the hospital I was placed in this service, with the rank of captain. After a varied experience I was provided with an expired furlough and a military order offering $50 reward for my apprehension as a deserter. With these in hand I was commanded to present myself at the Federal camp at the head of Choctawhatchie Bay, above Barrancas, and was welcomed heartily.

Here my work began, and I made the acquaintance of a genial sergeant of Co. B, Seventh Vermont Volunteers, and a warm friendship grew up between us. I was accorded free access to the Pensacola Navy Yard, and the Federal gunboats, and old Fort Pickens, and by keeping my eyes and ears open soon possessed valuable information, which I managed to communicate to Gen. D. H. Maury, at Mobile. Among other things I learned that a paymaster was shortly expected with funds for all troops in New Orleans and the Mississippi River and the men on the gunboat fleet, and the troops at Barrancas, and the men at work in the navy yard.

A plan was devised by Gen. Maury to capture the paymaster and his funds. A plan was also devised by Col. Page Baker, now editor-in-chief of the Times-Democrat, who was to make an attack from the open sea in the dead of night, on Fort Pickens, taking his men there in boats from the Perdido river. Col. Baker had nearly 200 picked men for this service, which he was to command, and which he believes yet would have been successful, but Gen. Maury would not give his consent at the hour for Col. Baker's departure.

But I am getting away from my subject. My part in Gen. Maury's plan was to set fire to the powder magazine and under cover of the resulting confusion of the explosion, the Confederates were to make the attack. The firing of a pistol beyond the picket line near the Light House was to apprise me that General Maury was ready to perform his part of the programme.

Well, on the fateful night I and my friend, the Vermont sergeant, spent part of the night over a bottle of wine. I had prepared a ball of twine, which, steeped in turpentine, I intended to use in blowing up the magazine. Along about 11:00 o'clock we bade one another good night. I had turned the hands of the sergeant's watch up about an hour and a half, and he thought it was nearing 1:00 a. m. I left the sergeant's tent, and a few moments afterwards I heard a pistol shot, apparently at the place agreed upon as my signal. I hastily got my ball of twine, and going to within a short distance of the magazine, lighted it and hurled it at the magazine. Just as I threw it I saw a sentinel not fifteen feet away. He saw the deed, and jumping to the burning ball he threw it toward me and then fired at me as I fled. That bullet passed so close to my head that it raised a blister on my right ear. A burning cigar would have accomplished the purpose designed, whereas the blaze failed. I afterwards found that General Maury had given up the attack as too dangerous, when too late to give me notice.

Well, I ran to Warrington, where I went to the house of a friend, whose name I have forgotten. He was a true Southerner, but employed at the navy yard. The sentinel had gotten a fairly good view of my face as the light flared when I lighted the ball of cord, and of course, details of soldiers were out looking for me. I remained at the house of my friend for three days, but realizing that he would be placed in a very compromising position if I was found there, I decided to make a dash for liberty, and the fourth night I tried to escape to the Confederate lines, but was captured and taken to the encampment of the Seventh Vermont Regiment of Infantry near to Fort Barrancas.

There was where I had the experience of being hanged. A crowd of infuriated soldiers surrounded me, and realizing that they had captured a Confederate spy, proceeded to hang me without further ado. A rope was slipped around my neck and the other end was placed over a projecting beam of a building over which they pulled me up by hand, until I was about a finger's length above the earth I could touch the ground with my toes, however, and this I was doing when discovered in the act by one of the Yanks. To remedy this defect the executioners scooped a hole in the sand with their hands sufficient to let my body swing free and it was then that I choked into a state of insensibility. When life was nearly extinct the Vermont sergeant, having been called, ran up and interfered, and ordered my body to be taken down, insisting that I was the wrong man. Restoratives were applied, and by vigorous friction I was resuscitated.

"But tell me the sensations you felt when you were hanged," requested the reporter.

The first sensation, replied Mr. Mann, was as near like that of a steam boiler ready to explode as anything I can call to mind. Every vein and blood vessel leading to and from the heart seemed to be charged with an oppressive fullness that must find an avenue of escape or explode. The nervous system throughout its length was tingling with a painful, pricking sensation, the like of which I never felt before or since. Then followed the sense of an explosion, as if a volcano had erupted. This seemed to give me relief, and the sensation of pain gave way slowly to a pleasurable feeling — a feeling much to be desired by everyone could it be arrived at without hanging. With this sensation a light broke in upon my sight resembling a milky whiteness, yet strange to say, so transparent that it was easier to pierce with the eye than the light of day. Then there came into my mouth a taste of sweetness the like of which I have never since known. Then I felt as though I was moving on, and leaving something behind — a weight — a hindrance * * * a consciousness which seemed to say good-bye to the body. I wandered on, but how far, as to the yardstick, I could not say, but I came to an immense wall.

Beyond that wall I heard music, the most entrancing I ever listened to — I several times counted to be sure that I heard twenty-two separate parts to the same tune, and it seemed that more than a thousand harps led in each part, accompanied by myriads of voices, and I recognized, I think, the old much-loved tune, "All Hail the Power of Jesus Name," as the leading part of their music.

Yes, those are some of the sensations I felt when I was hanged, and as I was hearing this sweet music I think they let me down.

Now, what is the sensation of coming back to life? asked the reporter.

Just as painful as those experienced when being hanged, replied Mr. Mann. It was acute torture, a torture so excruciating as to tempt man to circle the moon and put out the light of the stars, rather than endure it. Every nerve seemed to have a pain of its own. My nose and finger ends seemed to be the seats of the most excruciating agony of all. In half an hour the pain was all over, and I would not go through it again for the wealth of the Indies.

...

You ask, "What happened afterwards?"

Well, I was court-martialed and came free.

You see the sentinel swore that it was about 11:30 o'clock at night when he saw me attempt to blow up the powder magazine, but the sergeant swore that I was with him until nearly 1:00 o'clock a. m. in his tent. He swore truthfully, according to his watch, for I had turned it ahead two hours.

"Did the sergeant's testimony relieve you of suspicion after you were acquitted?" asked the reporter.

Upon the word of that sergeant all suspicion of guilt was removed from the minds of those who knew him well. But when a dog has earned a hard name he is never forgiven. And the same is true of any man with a stain upon his name. It is wiped off by a long life of irreproachable conduct. Every eye that looked upon me seemed to say "guilty."

You ask me "How long did I remain in the Federal lines after the court martial?"

It was less than a week; four days perhaps.

"How did you escape? Was leaving their camp not surrounded with danger?"

Yes, I was conscious that an open eye was upon me all the time. This gave me more concern for my future than I felt when the rope was on my neck...

Sol. Smith, who previous to the war had been upon the detective force of Pensacola, had been made Gen. Maury's chief scout. He had free access to their camps; could pass in and out at pleasure as a huckster. I entrusted every item of information to him for delivery. He was an "Underground-grape-vine-telegram" between myself and Gen. Maury.

Anticipating his arrival, and by putting two and two together, I had made my conclusions this way: That if we were seen to meet and speak, that both of us would be suspicioned, thrown into prison, and executed upon a very slender thread of circumstantial evidence. My conclusions were correct. As soon as he appeared in camp I was conscious that the number of eyes watching me were doubled. In spite of my efforts to evade him, he ran me down, and his first words were almost fatal. He saw the effects of his words upon me and his mistake then dawned upon him, but his ready wit apparently turned down any cause for suspicion. We separated until after sun set, and met out beyond the drill ground among some small, thorny, scrubby brush — a peculiar growth in that locality. We discovered that six men with guns were coming our way. To be overtaken meant our capture, or a duel unto death, because both were well armed. It was not safe for us to exchange shots, unless sure of our escape from them.

We were near the line of pickets that extended a mile in length across the neck of the peninsula from the Gulf to an inlet. There was too much of daylight to try to force our way across their line safely. There were four gate-ways of escape between which to choose. One was across the neck of land to the Inlet, which opened into Pensacola Bay. It could be forded at low tide. We could make a run for that place, but it was a public resort for idle crocodiles. A rifle pit for the pickets extended from the Light House to the Inlet. A stretch of white sand forty yards wide lay between the Inlet and highland and a man was a fair mark night or day on that sand. Another route was an open road passing by the Light House, and the last choice was by the Gulf shore.

Escaping our pursuers to give us time to consider which of these gates we would select was the important thought at that moment. Those scrubby thorn bushes curiously bent their limbs in an arch to the sand. Two of them near each other would afford a small man cover in the darkness. We found such bushes as we needed as twilight was fast fading out. We went under them, taking our chances of elusion, or discovery and a duel. Our pursuers followed us by our tracks in the sand to near where we were. We listened to their talk as they passed on by us and returned. When we knew that they had abandoned pursuit we felt assured of our escape from their lines that night.

Having now a bit of leisure we canvassed all avenues that were open for our departure. Crocodiles are said to regard the flesh of a white man as the most dainty morsel. We therefore declined to invade their territory. We preferred to fight our equals in the open at places of our own choosing. We also declined the sandy margin at the Inlet. I preferred to take chances of running the gauntlet by the Light House. Smith declined that route, for it was the guardsman's headquarters and all of them on the line reclined there when off duty. Then only the margin by the gulf was open as a last choice. There was a bank slightly higher than a man's head along the Gulf shore. One sentry's beat of about thirty steps lay along this sea front on this bank. "By stealthy approaches we can make our way to the shoulder of the bank when the sentry turns to re-walk his beat. The roar of waves breaking on the sand will be much in our favor. I will fix this bayonet on a pike, and as the sentry turns, I will wound him by a heavy jab in his ribs, and then we can run for safety," said my friend Smith. A bit of practice made Smith's plans a success. We had run a hundred yards, perhaps, when we heard a call of distress, saying: "Corporal of the guard, post number two, run here quick." We did not tarry to learn what he wanted in his call of distress. It was now nearly 3 o'clock in the morning. It was seven miles up the Perdido River to where Smith's brother-in-law lived. We made our way there and waited for breakfast and then went on, as we did not desire to linger near where Federal cavalry scouts might appear.

We were two miles away on our journey, when the sound of yelping dogs caught our ears. Smith's words were full of meaning when he said: "Mann, our safety lies in a successful run of three miles up the river to an old mill seat; my boat is there and if we can reach there in time we can row out in the river beyond gunshot range or we will have to hide in the hollow of a big cypress which stands out in the water away from the shore." When we got there the boat was gone. "We must swim to the opposite side of that cypress, and not be slow about it," said Smith. "I cut out a door in that tree on the water front and fixed a seat in it so that I could set on it and catch fish. We will be safe from their sight in there."

"Did the dogs not follow you in the water and disclose your hiding place?" asked the reporter.

"Yes, they came right in, and if they could have spoken they would have told. The 'gaters took one of the dogs down unto themselves and the other two were called out of the water. After the Yanks tried their marksmanship on some ducks away out in the river, they returned to their camp, leaving us undisturbed by their presence.

"That was the most welcome thing coming your way for several hours," suggested the reporter.

Indeed it was! Perhaps an hour after their departure, Smith and I were discussing the possibility of our escape from the 'gaters, that were holding us prisoners in our retreat — a dozen or more. Our talk was interrupted by a peculiar noise, low, but distinct. It was a well known countersign to Smith, by which to recognize a friend when it was made. Smith answered the signal in low and cautious tones, saying: "Is that you, Ben?" The answer came back, asking: "Is that you, Sam?" By this time Smith had recognized the voice of his cousin, another one of Col. Harry Maury's scouts. "Hello Ned! you are the most welcome man alive!" said Smith. "I and the man I went to relieve at Barrancas are here. The Yanks run us into this tree and the 'gaters have kept us here. We are glad to have you come!

"Well, get in the boat. You did not return as soon as I expected. I took your boat and went after these fine trout to sell to the Yanks, while I was looking after your safety. We had better row up to the mouth of Hurrican creek, where some of Col. Harry's cavalry have been awaiting our arrival," said Ned. The cavalry had gone when we landed. We made a fire and roasted the fish in their jackets. We gathered some grains of corn the horses had wasted while eating. These we roasted also, and of the roasted fish and corn we made our dinner. We felt safe in taking an hour for sleep before resuming our journey to Col. Maury's camp at Bluff Springs.

A Nurse Turned Spy

Sarah Emma Edmonds dressed as a man so that she could join the Union Army, where she served as male nurse for a time. When the opportunity arose to volunteer as a spy, she jumped at the chance, and made several trips behind Confederate lines in disguise. Here is her account[6] of one of those trips...

Sara Emma Edmonds, dressed as male nurse, "Frank Thompson."

Now a new disguise was necessary, and I decided to abandon the African relation, and assume that of the Hibernian. Having had this in view before leaving Williamsburg, I procured the dress and outfit of an Irish female peddler, following the army, selling cakes, pies, etc., together with a considerable amount of brogue, and a set of Irish phrases, which did much toward characterizing me as one of the "rale ould stock of bog-trotters."

The bridges were not finished across the Chickahominy when I was ready to cross the river, so I packed up my new disguise in my cake and pie basket, and my horse, "Frank," and I took a bath in the cool water of the Chickahominy. After

---

[6] Taken from *Nurse and Spy in the Union Army: Comprising the Adventures and Experiences of a Woman in Hospitals, Camps, and Battle-Fields,* 1865.

swimming my noble steed across the river, I dismounted, and led him to the edge of the water — gave him a farewell pat, and let him swim back again to the other side, where a soldier awaited his return. It was now evening; I did not know the precise distance to the enemy's picket line, but thought it best to avoid the roads, and consequently I must spend the night in the swamp, as the only safe retreat. It required some little time to don my new disguise, and feel at home in the clothes. I thought the best place for my debut was the "Chickahominy swamp." I did not purpose, this time, to pass the enemy's lines in the night, but to present myself at the picket line, at a sea-sonable hour, and ask admission as one of the fugitives of that section flying from the approach of the Yankees, which was a usual thing.

In crossing the river I had my basket strapped on my back, and did not know that all it contained was completely drenched, until I required to use its contents. It was, therefore, with feelings of dread and disappointment that I discovered this sad fact, for I had been suffering from slight ague [fever] chills during the day, and feared the consequences of spending the night in wet clothing, especially in that malaria-infested region. However, there was no alternative, and I was obliged to make the best of it. I had brought a patch-work quilt with me from the hospital, but that, too, was wet. Yet it kept off some of the chill night air, and the miasmatic breath of that "dismal swamp." The remembrance of the sufferings of that night seem to be written upon my memory "as with a pen of iron."

...

That night I was attacked by severe chills—chills beyond description, or even conception, except by those who have experienced the freezing sensation of a genuine ague chill. During the latter part of the night the other extreme presented itself, and it seemed as if I should roast alive, and not a single drop of water to cool my parched tongue; it was enough to make any one think of the "rich man" of the Bible, and in sympathy with his feelings cry to "Father Abraham" for assistance. My mind began to wander, and I became quite delirious. There seemed to be the horrors of a thousand deaths concentrated around me; I was tortured by fiends of every conceivable shape and magnitude. Oh, how it makes me shudder to recall the scenes which my imagination conjured up during those dark weary hours! Morning at last came, and I was aroused from the horrible night-mare which had paralyzed my senses through the night, by the roar of cannon and the screaming of shell through the forest.

But there I was, helpless as an infant, equally unable to advance or retreat, without friend or foe to molest or console me, and nothing even to amuse me but my own thoughts. I looked upon the surrounding scenery, and pronounced it very unromantic; then my eye fell upon my Irish costume, and I began to remember the fine phrases which I had taken so much pains to learn, when the perfect absurdity of my position rushed over my mind with overwhelming force, and the ludicrousness of it made me, for the moment, forget my lamentable condition, and with one uncontrollable burst of laughter I made that swamp resound in a manner which would have done credit to a person under happier circumstances, and in a better state of health.

...

The cannonading was only the result of a reconnoissance, and in a few hours ceased altogether. But not so my fever and chills; they were my constant companions for two days and two nights in succession. At the end of that time I was an object of pity. With no medicine, no food, and consequently little strength; I was nearly in a state of starvation. My pies and cakes were spoiled in the basket, in consequence of the drenching they had received in crossing the river, and now I had no means of procuring more. But something must be done; I could not bear the thought of thus starving to death in that inglorious manner; better die upon the scaffold at Richmond, or be shot by the rebel pickets; anything but this. So I thought and said, as I rallied all my remaining strength to arrange my toilette preparatory to emerging from my concealment in the swamp.

It was about nine o'clock in the morning of the third day after crossing the river, when I started, as I thought, towards the enemy's lines, and a more broken-hearted, forlorn-looking "Bridget" never left "ould Ireland," than I appeared to be that morning. I traveled from that time until five o'clock in the afternoon, and was then deeper in the swamp than when I started. My head or brain was completely turned. I knew not which way to go, nor did I know east from west, or north from south.

It was a dark day in every sense of the word—and I had neither sun nor compass to guide me. At five o'clock the glorious booming of cannon reverberated through the dense wilderness, and to me, at that hour, it was the sweetest and most soul-inspiring music that ever greeted my ear. I now turned my face in the direction of the scene of action, and was not long in extricating myself from the desert which had so long enveloped me.

Soon after emerging from the swamp I saw, in the distance, a small white house, and thither I bent my weary footsteps. I found it deserted, with the exception of a sick rebel soldier, who lay upon a straw-tick on the floor in a helpless condition. I went to him, and assuming the Irish brogue, I inquired how he came to be left alone, and if I could render him any assistance. He could only speak in a low whisper, and with much difficulty, said he had been ill with typhoid fever a few weeks before, and had not fully recovered when General Stoneman attacked the rebels in the vicinity of Coal Harbor, and he was ordered to join his company. He participated in a sharp skirmish, in which the rebels were obliged to retreat; but he fell out by the way, and fearing to fall into the hands of the Yankees, he had crawled along as best he could, sometimes on his hands and knees, until he reached the house in which I found him.

He had not eaten anything since leaving camp, and he was truly in a starving condition. I did not dare say to him "ditto"—with regard to poor "Bridget's" case—but thought so, and realized it most painfully. He also told me that the family who had occupied the house had abandoned it since he came there, and that they had left some flour and corn-meal, but had not time to cook anything for him. This was good news for me, and exhausted as I was, I soon kindled a fire, and in less than fifteen minutes a large hoe-cake was before it in process of baking, and a sauce-pan of water heating, for there was no kettle to be found. After searching about the premises, I found some tea packed away in a small basket, with some earthearn ware, which the family had forgotten to take with them. My cake being cooked, and tea made, I fed the poor famished rebel as tenderly as if he had been my brother, and he seemed as grateful for my kindness, and thanked me with as much politeness, as if I had been Mrs. Jeff Davis. The next important item was to attend to the cravings of my own appetite, which I did without much ceremony.

After making my toilet and adjusting my wig in the most approved Irish style, I approached the sick man, and for the first time noticed his features and general appearance. He was a man about thirty years of age, was tall and had a slight figure, regular features, dark hair and large, mournful, hazel eyes; altogether he was a very pleasing and intelligent looking man. I thought him quite an interesting patient, and if I had had nothing more important to attend to, I should have enjoyed the privilege of caring for him until he recovered. It is strange how sickness and disease disarm our antipathy and remove our prejudices.

...

After studying my countenance a few moments he asked me to pray with him. I did not dare to refuse the dying man's request, nor did I dare to approach my Maker in an assumed tone of voice; so I knelt down beside him, and in my own natural voice breathed a brief and earnest prayer for the departing soldier, for grace to sustain him in that trying hour, and finally for the triumph of truth and right.

When I arose from my knees he grasped my hand eagerly and said: "Please tell me who you are. I cannot, if I would, betray you, for I shall very soon be standing before that God whom you have just addressed." I could not tell him the truth and I would not tell him a falsehood, so I evaded a direct reply, but promised that when he became stronger I would tell him my history. He smiled languidly and closed his eyes, as much as to say that he understood me.

...

I began to look around for something which I might convert into a light, but did not succeed in finding anything better than a piece of salt pork, which I fried, pouring the fat into a dish in which I put a cotton rag, and then lighting the end of the rag I found I had secured quite a respectable light. After making some corn-meal gruel for my patient, I took care to fasten the doors and windows so that no one could enter the house without my knowledge, and screened the windows so that no light might attract the rebel scouts.

Thus with a sort of feeling of security I took my seat beside the sick man. The dews of death were already gathering on his pallid brow. I took his hand in mine, examined his pulse again, and wiped the cold perspiration from his forehead.

...

Then he said, "I have a last request to make. If you ever pass through the Confederate camp between this and Richmond inquire for Major McKee, of General Ewell's staff, and give him a gold watch which you will find in my pocket; he will know what to do with it; and tell him I died happy, peacefully." He then told me his name and the regiment to which he had belonged. His name was Allen Hall. Taking a ring from his finger he tried to put it on mine, but his strength failed, and after a pause he said, "Keep that ring in memory of one whose sufferings you have alleviated, and whose soul has been refreshed by your prayers in the hour of dissolution." Then folding his hands together as a little child would do at its mother's knee, he smiled a mute invitation for prayer. After a few moments' agonizing prayer in behalf of that departing spirit, the dying man raised himself up in the bed and cried out with his dying breath, "Glory to God! Glory to God! I am almost home!"

He was almost gone. I gave him some water, raised the window, and using my hat for a fan, I sat down and watched the last glimmering spark of light go out from those beautiful windows of the soul. Putting his hand in mine he signed to me to raise his head in my arms. I did so, and in a few moments he ceased to breathe.

He died about twelve o'clock—his hand clasping mine in the painful grip of death, my arm supporting him, and his head leaning on my bosom like a wearied child. I laid him down, closed his eyes, and straightened his rigid limbs; then folding his hands across his breast, I drew his blanket close around him and left him in the silent embrace of death.

...

Perhaps some of my readers will pronounce me a stoic, entirely devoid of feeling, when I tell them that two hours after I wrapped the unconscious form of my late patient in his winding-sheet, I enveloped myself in my patchwork quilt, and laid me down not far from the corpse, and slept soundly until six o'clock in the morning. Feeling much refreshed I arose, and after spending a few moments by the side of my silent companion, contemplating the changes which the King of Terrors had wrought, I cut a lock of hair from his temple, took the watch and a small package of letters from his pocket, replaced the blanket reverently, and bade him farewell.

...

I then made the tour of the house from garret to cellar, to find all the household fixings which an Irishwoman would be supposed to carry with her in such an emergency—for I expected to be searched before I was admitted through the lines.

I packed both my baskets, for I had two now, and was ready for another start. But before leaving I thought best to bury my pistol and every article in my possession which could in any way induce suspicion. Then taking a farewell look at the beautiful features of the dead, I left the house, going directly the nearest road to the rebel picket line. I felt perfectly safe in doing so, for the rebel soldier's watch was a sufficient passport in daylight, and a message for Major McKee would insure me civility at least.

I followed the Richmond road about five miles before meeting or seeing any one. At length I saw a sentinel in the distance, but before he observed me I sat down to rest and prepare my mind for the coming interview. While thus waiting to have my courage reinforced, I took from my basket the black pepper and sprinkled a little of it on my pocket handkerchief, which I applied to my eyes. The effect was all I could have desired...

I now resumed my journey, and displayed a flag of truce, a piece of a cotton window curtain which I brought from the house at which I had stopped overnight. As I came nearer the picket-guard signaled to me to advance, which I did as fast as I could under the circumstances, being encumbered with two heavy baskets packed full of earthenware, clothing, quilts, etc. Upon coming up to the guard, instead of being dismayed at his formidable appearance, I felt rejoiced, for there stood before me an immense specimen of a jolly Englishman, with a blind smile on his good-natured face, provoked, I presume, by the supremely ludicrous figure I presented.

He mildly questioned me with regard to my hopes and fears, whence I came and whither I was going, and if I had seen any Yankees. My sorrowful story was soon told. My peppery handkerchief was freely applied to my eyes, and the tears ran down my face without the least effort on my part. The good-natured guard's sympathy was excited, more especially as I was a foreigner like himself, and he told me I could pass along and go just wherever I pleased, so far as he was concerned...

...

After thanking the picket-guard for his kindness, I went on my way toward the rebel camp. I had not gone far when the guard called me back and advised me not to stay in camp overnight, for, said he, "One of our spies has just come in and reported that the Yankees have finished the bridges across the Chickahominy, and intend to attack us either to-day or to-night, but Jackson and Lee are ready for them." He went on to tell me how many masked batteries they had prepared, and said he, "There is one," pointing to a brush-heap by the road-side, "that will give them fits if they come this way."

Feeling somewhat in a hurry, I started once more for camp. I concluded after getting through the lines that I could dispense with one of my baskets, so setting one of them down under a tree I felt much more comfortable, and was not quite so conspicuous an object going into camp. I went directly to headquarters and inquired for Major McKee. I was told that he would not be there before evening, and my informant drawled out after me, "He's gone to set a trap for the d—d Yankees."

...

There was no difficulty in finding out the force of the enemy or their plans for the coming battle, for everyone, men and women, seemed to think and talk of nothing else.

Five o'clock came, and with it Major McKee. I lost no time in presenting myself before his majorship, and with a profound Irish courtesy I made known my business, and delivered the watch and package. I did not require any black pepper now to assist the lachrymal glands in performing their duty, for the sad mementoes which I had just delivered to the major so forcibly reminded me of the scenes of the past night that I could not refrain from weeping. The major, rough and stern as he was, sat there with his face between his hands and sobbed like a child. Soon he rose to his feet, surveyed me from head to foot, and said, "You are a faithful woman, and you shall be rewarded."

He then asked: "Can you go direct to that house, and show my men where Allen's body is?" I answered in the affirmative—whereupon he handed me a ten dollar Federal bill, saying, as he did so: "If you succeed in finding the house, I will give you as much more." I thanked him, but positively declined taking the money. He did not seem to understand the philosophy of a person in my circumstances refusing money, and when I looked at him again his face wore a doubtful, puzzled expression, which alarmed me. I was actually frightened, and bursting into a passionate fit of weeping, I exclaimed vehemently: "Oh, Gineral, forgive me! but me conshins wud niver give me pace in this world nor in the nixt, if I wud take money for carying the dyin missage for that swate boy that's dead and gone—God rest his soul. Och, indade, indade I nivir cud do sich a mane thing, if I im a poor woman." The major seemed satisfied, and told me to wait until he returned with a detachment of men.

When he returned with the men, I told him that I did not feel able to walk that distance, and requested him to let me have a horse, stating the fact that I had been sick for several days, and had slept but little the night before. He did not answer a word, but ordered a horse saddled immediately, which was led forward by a colored boy, who assisted me to mount. I really felt mean, and for the first time since I had acted in the capacity of spy, I despised myself for the very act which I was about to perform. I must betray the confidence which that man reposed in me. He was too generous to harbor a suspicion against me, and thus furnished me the very means of betraying him.

This feeling did not last long, however, for as we started on our mission he said to his men: "Now, boys, bring back the body of Captain Hall, if you have to walk through Yankee blood to the knees." That speech eased my conscience considerably. I was surprised to hear him say "Captain Hall," for I did not know until then that he was an officer. There was nothing about his uniform or person to indicate his rank, and I had supposed he was a private soldier.

We made our way toward the house very cautiously, lest we should be surprised by the Federals. I rode at the head of the little band of rebels as guide, not knowing but that I was leading them into the jaws of death every step we advanced, and if so it would probably be death for me as well as for them. Thus we traveled those five miles, silently, thoughtfully, and stealthily. The sun had gone down behind the western hills, and the deepening shadows were fast gathering around us as we came in sight of the little white cottage in the forest, where I had so recently spent such a strangely, awfully solemn night.

The little detachment halted to rest, and to make arrangements before approaching the house. This detachment consisted of twenty-four men, under a sergeant and a corporal. The men were divided into squads, each of which was to take its turn at carrying the body of their late Captain upon a stretcher, which they had brought for that purpose. As we drew near, and saw no sign of an approaching enemy, they regretted that they had not brought an ambulance; but I did not regret it, for the present arrangement suited me exactly. Having settled things satisfactorily among themselves, we again resumed our march and were soon at the gate. The sergeant then ordered the corporal to proceed to the house with a squad of men and bring out the corpse, while he stationed the remaining men to guard all the approaches to the house.

He then asked me to ride down the road a little way, and if I should see or hear anything of the Yankees to ride back as fast as possible and let them know. I assented, and joyfully complied with the first part of his request. This was a very pleasant duty assigned me, for which I mentally thanked the sergeant a thousand times. I turned and rode slowly down the road, but not "seeing or hearing anything of the Yankees," I thought it best to keep on in that direction until I did. I was like the zouave, after the battle of Bull Run, who said he was ordered to retreat, but not being ordered to halt at any particular place, he preferred to keep on until he reached New York. So I preferred to keep on until I reached the Chickahominy, where I reported progress to the Federal general.

I had no desire to have that little escort captured, and consequently said nothing about it in my report; so the sergeant, with his men, were permitted to return to the rebel camp unmolested, bearing with them the remains of their beloved captain. After getting out of sight of the rebel guards, I made that horse go over the ground about as fast, I think, as he ever did before—which seemed to give him a bad impression of Yankees in general, and of me in particular, for ever after that night, it was as much as a person's life was worth to saddle him; at every attempt he would kick and bite most savagely.

CHAPTER FOUR

*A BULLET THROUGH MY HAIR, A BULLET THROUGH
MY TROUSERS*

— WARREN OLNEY: AT SHILOH —

Warren Olney lived an interesting life. He was born
and raised in Iowa, and his first job was as a school
teacher in Pella, Iowa. During his time there, one of
the students in his school was a boy destined to become a hero of the
Old West, Wyatt Earp.

When the Civil War broke out, Olney enlisted as a Private in
the 3rd Regiment of Iowa Infantry. In 1864, he was commissioned as
a Captain of the 2nd Regiment of Missouri Colored Infantry, and he
held that position until the end of the war.

After the war, he became a lawyer and moved to California to
practice law. There he became a founding member of the Sierra
Club, and wrote the organization's first charter.

From 1903 to 1905, he served as the 34th Mayor of Oakland, California. During his time as Mayor, he felt that the community needed
a secure water supply. To accomplish this goal, he supported the
damming of the Tuolumne River to create the Hetch Hetchy Reservoir. The Sierra Club was opposed to the Reservoir, but Olney
thought it was necessary and continued to support the project until

his death. This action on his part led to his ouster from the Sierra Club, and the loss of many of the friendships he had created there.

Olney saw very little action during the Civil War, but he did take part in the Battle of Shiloh. This is his account[7] of that battle, told from his perspective as a lowly Private.

Prelude to Battle

Private Olney describes his experience early in the war, the buildup of the Union Army at Pittsburg Landing, and how totally unprepared the Army was for the impending Confederate attack.

Very interesting descriptions of the great battles of the late war, written by prominent generals, have been lately published and widely read. It seems to me, however, that it is time for the private soldier to be heard from.

Of course, his field of vision is much more limited than that of his general. On the other hand, it is of vital importance to the latter to gloss over his mistakes, and draw attention only to those things which will add to his reputation. The private soldier has no such feeling. It is only to the officers of high rank engaged that a battle can bring glory and renown. To the army of common soldiers, who do the actual fighting, and risk mutilation and death, there is no reward except the consciousness of duty bravely performed. This was peculiarly the case in the late war, when more than a million of young men, the flower of our country, left their workshops and farms, their schools and colleges, to endure the hardships of the march and the camp, to risk health, limb and life, that

---

[7] Taken from *"Shiloh" As Seen By A Private Soldier*, by Warren Olney, 1889.

their country might live, expecting nothing, hoping nothing for themselves, but all for their fatherland.

The first really great battle of the war was that of Pittsburg Landing, or Shiloh, and I shall not only attempt to give a general account of the battle, but also describe it from the point of view of a man in the ranks.

...

At this time the Third Iowa Infantry was strung along the North Missouri Railroad, guarding bridges and doing other police work. Company B, which had the honor of having on its muster roll private Olney, was stationed at that time in the little town of Sturgeon, Missouri, where our principal occupation was to keep from freezing. We had then spent eight months campaigning in that border State — that is, if you call guarding railways and bridges, and attempting to overawe the disaffected, enlivened now and then by a brisk skirmish, campaigning. The Second Iowa had led the charge which captured the hostile breastworks at Donelson, and General Grant had telegraphed to General Halleck at St. Louis, who had repeated the message to the Governor of our State, that the Second Iowa was the bravest of the brave. The First Iowa had distinguished itself at Wilson's Creek, near Springfield, under General Lyon, while we — well, we hadn't done much of anything but to get a licking at Blue Mills. Therefore, when a message to move came, and we found ourselves on the way to join General Grant's army, we felt quite hilarious.

At St. Louis we were put on board the steamer "Iatan." Down the Mississippi, up the Ohio, up the Tennessee. As we proceeded up the Tennessee we were continually overtaking or being joined by other steamboats loaded with troops, until presently the river was alive with transports, carrying the army of the West right into the heart of the Confederacy. It was a beautiful and stirring sight; mild weather had set in (it was now the second week of March), the flotilla of steamboats, black with soldiers, bands playing, flags flying, all combined to arouse and interest. It was the "pomp and circumstance of glorious war."

Frequent stoppages were made, giving us a chance to run ashore. About the thirteenth we reached the landing-place, which soon afterwards became famous. The river was very high, and at first there seemed to be doubts as to where a landing should be effected, but in a few days the question was settled. Our boat was moored as near the shore as possible, and we joined the immense throng painfully making their way through the unfathomable mud to camps in the dense woods. The first things I observed after reaching the high bluff, were trees that had been torn and shattered by shells from our gunboats, which, it seems, had dislodged a company of Confederates, who had dug rifle-pits on the bluff, from whence they had fired on our steamboats.

...

The mud — well, it was indescribable. Though we were only a mile from our base of supplies, the greatest difficulty was experienced in getting camp equipage and provisions. We found that other divisions of the army had landed before us, moving farther out to the front towards Corinth, and had so cut up the roads that they were quagmires their whole length. Teams were stalled in the mud in every direction. The principal features of the landscape were trees, mud, wagons buried to the hub, and struggling, plunging mule teams. The shouts of teamsters and resounding whacks filled the air; and as to profanity — well, you could see the air about an enraged teamster turn blue as he exhorted his impenitent mules. And the rain! how it did come down! As I recall it, the spring of 1862 did not measure its rainfall in Western Tennessee by inches, but by feet.

But in time our camp was fairly established. Sibley tents were distributed, one for fourteen men. They protected us from the rain, but they had their drawbacks. Several of us were schoolmates from a Western college, and, of course, in some respects, constituted a little aristocracy. We had had a small tent to ourselves, and the socialistic grayback, as yet, had not crawled therein. Now, we were required to share our tent with others, and that might mean a great many. But when it came to a question of sleeping out in the cold rain, or camping down in a crowded tent in true democratic equality and taking the chances of immigration from our neighbors' clothing, we did not prefer the rain.

...

Our regiment was brigaded with the Twenty-eighth, Thirty-second, and Forty-first Illinois. The division was commanded by Brigadier-General Stephen A. Hurlbut (since somewhat noted as United States Minister to Peru). We had served under him in Missouri, and our principal recollection of him was an event which occurred at Macon. We had got aboard a train of cattle cars for the purpose of going to the relief of some point threatened by the enemy. After waiting on the train two or three hours, expecting every moment to start, we noticed a couple of staff officers supporting on each side the commanding general, and leading him to the car I was in. Getting him to the side of the car, they boosted him in at the door, procured a soldier's knapsack for him to sit on, and left him. He was so drunk he couldn't sit upright. The consequence was that the regimental officers refused to move. A court-martial followed, and we heard no more of our general until we found him at Pittsburg Landing in command of a division. He showed so much coolness and bravery in the battle which followed, that we forgave him his first scandalous appearance. But the distrust of him before the battle can readily be imagined.

No one who has not been through the experience can realize the anxiety of the private soldier respecting the character and capacity of his commanding officer. His life is in the general's hand. Whether he shall be uselessly sacrificed, may depend wholly upon the coolness or readiness for an emergency of the commander; whether he has had two drinks or three; whether he has had a good night's rest, or a good cigar. The private soldier regards a new and unknown commander very much as a slave does a new owner, and with good reason. Without confidence on the part of the rank and file, victory is impossible. Their soldiers' confidence in Stonewall Jackson and Lee doubled the effective strength of their armies. When in the Franco-Prussian war a German regiment was called upon for a charge, each man felt that the order was given because it was necessary, and that what he was doing was part of a comprehensive scheme, whose success might very likely depend upon whether he did his assigned part manfully. The French soldier in that war had no such feeling and, of course, the result of that campaign was not long in doubt. In Napoleon's time, the confidence of the rank and file was such that time and again he was saved from defeat by the feeling of the attacked corps or detachment that it must hold its ground, or probably imperil the army. Oh, the sickening doubt and distrust of our generals during the first years of the war! Our soldiers were as brave as ever trod the earth, and thoroughly imbued with the cause for which they were fighting; but the suspicion that at headquarters there might be inefficiency or drunkenness; that marches and counter-marches had no definite purpose; that their lives might be uselessly thrown away—you would have to go through it to realize it! At the beginning of the war, the Southerners had a vast advantage over us in that respect. Generally speaking, they started out with the same able commanders they had at the end.

...

Troops were continually arriving, some of them freshly recruited, and not yet familiar with their arms, or the simplest elements of regimental maneuvers. It was said there were some regiments who had just received their guns, and had never fired them. Badeau says they came on the field without cartridges. I know that improved rifles were scarce, for my own regiment at that time did not have rifles, but old smooth bore muskets with buck-and-ball ammunition—that is, the cartridge had next to the powder a large ball, and then next to it three buck shot. Of course, we should have had no show against rifles at long range, but at short range, in woods and brush, these weapons were fearfully destructive, as we shall presently see.

Strange to say, these freshly recruited regiments were assigned to Sherman's division and to Prentiss' division, whose camps were scattered in the woods farthest out towards Corinth. As might have been expected, these new soldiers did not stand on the order of their going, when they suddenly discovered a hostile army on top of them.

A map of the place selected for the concentration of our army shows that with proper precautions and such defensive works as, later in the war, would have been constructed within a few hours, the place was impregnable. The river which ran in the rear was controlled by our gunboats, and furnished us the means of obtaining abundant supplies. Creeks with marshy banks protected either flank. The only possible avenue of attack upon this position was directly in front, and across that ran little creeks and ravines, with here and there open fields affording fine vantage-ground. A general anticipating the possibility of attack, would not have scattered his divisions so widely, and would have marked a line of defense upon which the troops should rally. Advantage would have been taken of the ground, and trees felled with the tops outwards, through which an attacking force would have, with great difficulty, to struggle. And later in the war, as a matter of precaution, and because of the proximity of the enemy, breastworks would have been thrown up. All this could have been done in a few hours. Our flanks were so well protected that no troops were needed there, and in case of attack, each division commander should have had his place in the front, to which to immediately march his command; while, the line being not more than three miles long at the very outside estimate, there were abundant forces to man it thoroughly, leaving a large force in the reserve to reinforce a point imperiled.

Why was not this done? It is hard to find an answer. General Sherman's division was at the extreme front. It was being organized. The enemy was not more than twenty-two miles away, and was known to be concentrating from all the West. Yet this general, who afterwards acquired such fame as a consummate master of the art of war, took no precautions whatever, not even thoroughly scouting the ground in his front. His pickets could not have been out more than a mile. General

Prentiss' division was also in process of organization, and he, like Sherman, was in advance, and on Sherman's left. The complete absence of the ordinary precautions, always taken by military commanders since the beginning of history, is inexplicable. The only reason I can conjecture for it grows out of the character of General Grant and his distinguished subordinate, and their inexperience. They had had then little practical knowledge of actual warfare. General Sherman, except on one occasion, had never heard a hostile gun fired. They had to learn their art, and the country and their army had to pay the cost of their teaching. Happily, they were able to profit by every lesson, and soon had no equals among our commanders. But because they have since deserved so well of their country, is no reason why history should be silent as to their mistakes. The Confederates would have made a great mistake in attacking us at all in such a position, if we had been prepared to receive them. But this want of preparation prevented us from taking advantage of the opportunity, and inflicting a crushing defeat upon the South. By it the war was prolonged, and every village and hamlet in the West had its house of mourning.

Immediately in the right rear of General Sherman was camped the veteran division of General McClernand. About two miles further back, and about a mile from the river, was stationed the reserve, consisting of two divisions, Hurlbut's and W. H. L. Wallace's, formerly C. F. Smith's. Across Owl Creek, and seven or eight miles off, was camped General Lew Wallace's division. It was so far away as not to be in easy supporting distance.

On April 1st, our division was marched to an open field, and there carefully reviewed by General Grant. This was our first sight of the victor of Donelson. Friday, the 4th of April, was a sloppy day, and just before sundown we heard firing off towards Sherman's division. We fell into line and started toward the front. After we had marched about a mile, pitch darkness came on. Presently, a staff officer directed a countermarch back to camp, saying it was only a rebel reconnoisance. It was a nasty march back in the mud, dense woods, and thick darkness.

All this day the Confederate army was struggling through the woods and mud, on its march from Corinth to attack us. It was the expectation of General Johnston and his subordinates to cover the intervening space between the two armies in this one day and attack early Saturday morning; but the difficulties of the march was such, that he did not make more than half the distance, and had to go into camp for the night. Saturday was a reasonably pleasant day, but General Johnston's troops had got so entangled in the forests, he did not feel justified in attacking until all his preparations were made, which took the whole of Saturday. He then moved up to within a mile or two of Sherman and Prentiss, and went into camp within sound of our drums.

The delay had been so great that Beauregard now advised a countermarch back to Corinth. He represented that our forces had surely been appraised of their march, and it would be too late now to effect a surprise; that they would undoubtedly find us all prepared, and probably behind breastworks and other obstructions. General Johnston was smarting under the criticisms of the campaign which resulted in the loss of Donelson. His courage and military instinct told him that now was the time to strike. He felt, too, that a bold stroke was necessary to redeem the fortunes of the Confederacy and his own reputation. His resolution was to conquer or die; and he replied to Beauregard: "We shall attack at daylight tomorrow."

Here was an army of a little over 40,000 men, as brave as ever shouldered muskets, fighting on their own soil, and, as they believed, for homes and liberty, resting for the night at about two miles from the invading army, and all prepared to attack at dawn, and sweep the invaders of their country back into the Tennessee river. Upon the favoring breeze, the sound of our drums at evening parade came floating to their ears. They heard the bugle note enjoying quiet and repose in the camp of their unsuspecting foe. They, themselves, were crouching in the thick woods and darkness, all prepared to spring on their prey. No camp-fire was lighted; no unnecessary sound was permitted; but silent, watchful, with mind and heart prepared for conflict, the Southern hosts waited for the morning.

Such was the situation, so far as our enemies were concerned. But how was it with the army fighting for the integrity and preservation of the nation? Let us begin with the commanding General. That day (Saturday) he dispatched General Halleck as follows: "The main force of the army is at Corinth. * * * The number at Corinth and within supporting distance of it cannot be far from 80,000 men." Later in the day he dispatched the news of the enemy's reconnoisance the night before, and added: "I have scarcely the faintest idea of an attack (general one) being made upon us, but will be prepared should a thing take place."

Grant had less than 50,000 men fit for battle. He thinks the enemy at Corinth, twenty-two miles away, has 80,000 men. He must know that the enemy knows Buell, with his army, will soon reach the Tennessee, and when united with his own will nearly double his effective strength; that now, and before Buell joins him, if ever, must the Confederates strike an effective blow. His pickets have been driven in the night before, the enemy using a piece or two of artillery; yet he does not expect an attack, and makes not the slightest preparation to receive or repel one. He leaves General Lew Wallace with over 7,000 good troops at Crump's Landing, out of easy supporting distance, Nelson's division and Crittenden's division of Buell's army at Savannah; and has no thought of moving them up that day to repel an overwhelming attack about to be made on him. On Saturday he visits his army and Sherman, and then goes back to Savannah, unsuspicious of the presence of the enemy.

How was it with General Sherman, who had the advance on the right, and was probably more relied upon by Grant and Halleck than was Prentiss? In fact it is not at all improbable that Grant wholly relied upon the two division commanders at the front, particularly Sherman, to keep him posted as to the movements of the hostile army. General Sherman reported on Saturday that he thought there were about two regiments of infantry and a battery of artillery about six miles out. As a matter of fact, the whole rebel army was not more than six miles out. Later in the day he dispatches: "The enemy is saucy, but got the worst of it yesterday, and will not press our pickets far. I do not apprehend anything like an attack on our position."

A tolerably extensive reading of campaigns and military histories justifies me in saying that such an exhibition of unsuspicious security in the presence of a hostile army is without a parallel in the history of warfare.

How was it with our army? We knew the enemy to be at Corinth, but there had been no intimation of advance; and no army could get over the intervening space in less than two days, of which, of course, it was the duty of our generals to have ample notice. Usually, before a battle, there seems to be something in the very air that warns the soldier and officer of what is coming, and to nerve themselves for the struggle; but most of us retired this Saturday night to our blankets in as perfect fancied security as ever enveloped an army.

But this was not true of all. A sense of uneasiness pervaded a portion of the advance line. Possibly there had been too much noise in the woods in front, possibly that occult sense, which tells us of the proximity of another, warned them of the near approach of a hostile army. Some of the officers noticed that the woods beyond the pickets seemed to be full of Rebel cavalry. General Prentiss was infected with this uneasiness, and at daylight on Sunday morning sent out the Twenty-first Missouri to make an observation towards Corinth.

This regiment, proceeding through the forest, ran plump upon the Confederate skirmish line, which it promptly attacked. Immediately the Missourians saw an army behind the skirmish line advancing upon them. They could hold their ground but for a moment. The enemy's advance swept them back, and, like an avalanche, the Confederate army poured into the camps of Sherman's and Prentiss' divisions.

The Attack

With the attack underway, confusion and panic spread through the Union camp. Olney goes on to tell of how the Union Army regrouped and settled in for a long day of fighting.

Battle of Shiloh (April 6-7, 1862).

At the first fire our men sprang to arms. By the time the enemy had reached our camps many regiments had become partially formed, but they were all unnerved by the shock. Some were captured by the enemy before they could get their clothes on. Some, without firing a shot, broke for the river-landing, three miles away, and cowered beneath its banks. General Sherman and his staff mounted their horses, and as they galloped past the Fifty-third Ohio, which was getting into line, one of the officers called out to him not to go any farther, for the rebel army was just beyond the rising ground. The general made use of some expression about not getting frightened at a reconnoisance, and went ahead. As he reached the slight elevation he beheld the Confederate army sweeping down upon him. Their skirmish line fired at him, killing his orderly. He realized at last that he was in the presence of a hostile army. From that moment he did everything that mortal man could do to retrieve his fatal mistake. Wounded twice, several horses successively killed under him, chaos and defeat all around, yet his clear intelligence and steady courage stamped him a born leader of men. The other generals and officers yielded to his superior force and obeyed his orders. He was everywhere, encouraging, threatening, organizing, and succeeded in establishing a tolerable line in the rear of his camps.

General Prentiss' troops were more demoralized than Sherman's. Whole regiments broke away, and were not reorganized until after the battle. A tide of fugitives set in toward the landing, carrying demoralization and terror with them.

Our camp was so far back that we heard nothing of this early uproar. The morning was a beautiful one, and after our early breakfast I started down the little creek, hunting for some first flowers of spring. I had scarcely got out of sight of camp, when the firing toward the front, though faintly heard, seemed too steady to be caused by the pernicious habit which prevailed of the pickets firing off their guns on returning from duty, preparatory to cleaning them. A sense of apprehension took possession of me. Presently artillery was heard, and then I turned toward camp, getting more alarmed at every step. When I reached camp a startled look was on every countenance. The musketry firing had become loud and general, and whole batteries of artillery were joining in the dreadful chorus. The men rushed to their tents and seized their guns, but as yet no order to fall in was given. Nearer and nearer sounded the din of a tremendous conflict. Presently the long roll was heard from the regiments on our right. A staff officer came galloping up, spoke a word to the Major in command, the order to fall in was shouted, the drummers began to beat the long roll, and it was taken up by the regiments on our left. The men, with pale faces, wild eyes, compressed lips, quickly accoutered themselves for battle. The shouts of the officers, the rolling of the drums, the hurrying to and fro of the men, the uproar of approaching but unexpected battle, all together produced sensations which cannot be described. Soon, teams with shouting drivers came tearing along the road toward the landing. Crowds of fugitives and men slightly wounded went hurrying past in the same direction. Uproar and turmoil were all around; but we, having got into line, stood quietly with scarcely a word spoken. Each man was struggling with himself and nerving himself for what bid fair to be a dreadful conflict. What thoughts of home and kindred and all that makes life dear come to one at such a moment.

Presently a staff officer rode up, the command to march was given, and with the movement came some relief to the mental and moral strain. As we passed in front of the Forty-first Illinois, a field officer of that regiment, in a clear, ringing voice, was speaking to his men, and announced that if any man left the ranks on pretense of caring for the wounded he should be shot on the spot; that the wounded must be left till the fight was over. His men cheered him, and we took up the cheer. Blood was beginning to flow through our veins again, and we could even comment to one another upon the sneaks who remained in camp, on pretense of being sick. As we moved toward the front the fugitives and the wounded increased in numbers. Poor wretches, horribly mutilated, would drop down, unable to go farther. Wagons full of wounded, filling the air with their groans, went hurrying by. As we approached the scene of conflict, we moved off to the left of the line of the rear-ward going crowd, crossed a small field and halted in the open woods beyond. As we halted, we saw right in front of us, but about three hundred or four hundred yards off, a dense line of Confederate infantry, quietly standing in ranks. In our excitement, and without a word of command, we turned loose and with our smooth bore muskets opened fire upon them. After three or four rounds, the absurdity of firing at the enemy at that distance with our guns dawned upon us, and we stopped. As the smoke cleared up we saw the enemy still there, not having budged or fired a shot in return. But though our action was absurd, it was a relief to us to do something, and we were rapidly becoming toned up to the point of steady endurance.

As we gazed at the enemy so coolly standing there, an Ohio battery of artillery came galloping up in our rear, and what followed I don't believe was equalled by anything of the kind during the war. As the artillery came up we moved off by the right flank a few steps, to let it come in between us and the Illinois regiment next on our left. Where we were standing was in open, low-limbed oak timber. The line of Southern infantry was in tolerably plain view through the openings in the woods, and were still standing quietly. Of course, we all turned our heads away from them to look at the finely equipped battery, as it came galloping from the rear to our left flank, its officers shouting directions to the riders where to stop their guns. It was the work of but an instant to bring every gun into position. Like a flash the gunners leaped from their seats and unlimbered the cannon. The fine six-horse teams began turning round with the caissons, charges were being rammed home, and the guns pointed toward the dense ranks of the enemy, when, from right in front, a dense puff of smoke, a tearing of shot and shell through the trees, a roar from half a dozen cannon, hitherto unseen, and our brave battery was knocked into smithereens. Great limbs of trees, torn off by cannon shot, came down on horse and rider, crushing them to earth. Shot and shell struck cannon, upsetting them; caissons exploded them. Not a shot was fired from our side.

But how those astounded artillery men — those of them who could run at all — did scamper out of there. Like Mark Twain's dog, they may be running yet. At least, it is certain that no attempt was ever made to reorganize that battery — it was literally wiped out then and there.

This made us feel mightily uncomfortable — in fact, we had been feeling quite uncomfortable all the morning. It did not particularly add to the cheerfulness of the prospect, to reflect that our division was the reserve of the army, and should not be called into action, ordinarily, until towards the close of the battle; while here we were, early in the forenoon, face to face with the enemy, our battery of artillery gobbled up at one mouthful, and the rest of the army in great strait, certainly, and probably demoralized.

One of the cannon shot had gone through our Colonel's horse, and the rider had been carried off the field. Colonel Pugh, of the Forty-first Illinois, then took command of the brigade, about-faced us, and marched us back across the little field, and halted us just behind the fence, the enemy during this maneuver leaving us wholly undisturbed.

The rails were thrown down and we lay flat upon the ground, while another battery came up and opened on the enemy, who had moved up almost to the wreck of our first battery.

Here, then, began a fierce artillery duel. Shot and shell went over us and crashing through the trees to the rear of us, and I suppose that shot and shell went crashing through the trees above the enemy; but if they didn't suffer any more from shot and shell than we did, there was a great waste of powder and iron that day. But how a fellow does hug the ground under such circumstances! As a shell goes whistling over him he flattens out, and presses himself into the earth, almost. Pity the sorrows of a big fat man under such a fire.

Later in the war we should have dug holes for ourselves with bayonets. We must have lain there hugging the ground for more than two hours, with now and then an intermission, listening to the flight of dreaded missiles above us; but, as nobody in our immediate neighborhood was hurt, we at length voted the performance of the artillery to be, on the whole, rather fine. During intermissions, while the scenes were shifting, as it were, we began to feel a disposition to talk and joke over the situation.

The reason why we were not subjected to an infantry fire, was because the enemy's forces, tangled in the wooded country, and in places beaten back by the stubborn gallantry of our surprised but not demoralized men, needed to be reorganized. All the Southern accounts agree that their brigades and divisions had become mixed in apparently hopeless confusion. The battlefield was so extensive that fighting was going on at some point all the time, so that at no time was there a complete cessation of the roar of artillery or the rattle of musketry.

Two or three times General Hurlbut came riding along our line; and once, during a lull, General Grant and staff came slowly riding by, the General with a cigar in his mouth, and apparently as cool and unconcerned as if inspection was the sole purpose of visiting us. The General's apparent indifference had, undoubtedly, a good influence on the men. They saw him undisturbed, and felt assured that the worst was over, and the attack had spent its force. This must have been soon after he reached the field; for, upon hearing the roar of battle in the morning at Savannah he went aboard a steamer, came up the river eight or nine miles, and did not reach the scene of action much, if any, before 10 o'clock. By that time, Sherman, McClernand and Prentiss had been driven more than a mile beyond their camps, and with such of their command as they could hold together had formed on the flanks of the two reserve divisions of Hurlbut and W. H. L. Wallace, who had moved forward beyond their own camps to meet them.

...

Fortunately for us, General Johnston's plan was to attack our left. If, when he was ready to renew the battle, he had assailed our right, where were Sherman's and McClernand's divisions, who had already done almost as much as flesh and blood could stand, nothing would have stopped him, and by two o'clock we should have been where we were at dark—that is, huddled about the landing. Then there would have been nothing to do but to surrender. Happily, most happily, when he renewed the assaults upon our lines, it was upon those portions manned by reserve divisions, troops that had not been seriously engaged, and had had time to steady their nerves, and to select favorable positions.

As for myself and comrades, we had become accustomed to the situation somewhat. The lull in the fighting in our immediate vicinity, and the reports which reached us that matters were now progressing favorably on the rest of the field, reassured us. We were becoming quite easy in mind. I had always made it a rule to keep a supply of sugar and some hard tack in my haversack, ready for an emergency. It stood me in good stead just then, for I alone had something besides fighting for lunch. I nibbled my hard tack, and ate my sugar with comfort and satisfaction, for I don't believe three men of our regiment were hurt by this artillery fire upon us, which had been kept up with more or less fury for two or three hours.

One of the little episodes of the battle happened about this time. We noticed that a Confederate, seated on one of the abandoned cannon I have mentioned, was leisurely taking an observation. He was out of range of our guns, but our First Lieutenant got a rifle from a man who happened to have one, took deliberate aim, and Johnny Reb tumbled.

But soon after noon the Confederate forces were ready to hurl themselves on our lines. There had been more or less fighting on our right all the time, but now Johnston had collected his troops and massed them in front of the Union army's left. Language is inadequate to give an idea of the situation. Cannon and musketry roared and rattled, not in volleys, but in one continual din. Charge after charge was made upon the Union lines, and every time repulsed. By concentrating the main body of his troops on our left, General Johnston was superior there to us in numbers, and there was no one upon whom we could call for help. General Lew Wallace had not taken the precaution to learn the roads between his division at Crump's Landing and the main body, and he and his 7,000 men were lost in the woods, instead of being where they could support us in this our dire extremity. The left wing of our brigade was the Hornet's Nest, mentioned in the Southern accounts of the battle. On the immediate right of my regiment was timber with growth of underbrush, and the dreadful conflict set the woods on fire, burning the dead and the wounded who could not crawl away. At one point not burned over, I noticed, after the battle, a strip of low underbrush which had evidently been the scene of a most desperate contest. Large patches of brush had been cut off by bullets at about as high as a man's waist, as if mowed with a scythe, and I could not find in the whole thicket a bush which had not at some part of it been touched by a ball. Of course, human beings could not exist in such a scene, save by closely hugging the ground, or screening themselves behind trees.

Hour after hour passed. Time and again the Confederate hordes threw themselves on our lines, and were repulsed; but our ranks were becoming dangerously thinned. If a few thousand troops could have been brought from Lew Wallace's division to our sorely-tried left the battle would have been won. His failure to reach us was fatal.

Yet, during all this terrible ordeal through which our comrades on the immediate right and the left of us were passing, we were left undisturbed until about two o'clock. Then there came from the woods on the other side of the field, to the edge of it, and then came trotting across it, as fine looking a body of men as I ever expect to see under arms. They came with their guns at what soldiers call right shoulder shift. Lying on the ground there, with the rails of the fence thrown down in front of us, we beheld them, as they started in beautiful line; then increasing their speed as they neared our side of the field, they came on till they reached the range of our smooth bore guns, loaded with buck and ball. Then we rose with a volley right in their faces. Of course, the smoke then entirely obscured the vision, but with eager, bloodthirsty energy, we loaded and fired our muskets at the top of our speed, aiming low, until, from not noticing any return fire, the word passed along from man to man to stop firing. As the smoke rose so that we could see over the field, that splendid body of men presented to my eyes more the appearance of a wind-row of hay than anything else. They seemed to be piled up on each other in a long row across the field. Probably the obscurity caused by the smoke, as well as the slight slope of the ground towards us, accounted for this piled up appearance, for it was something which could not possibly occur. But the slaughter had been fearful. Here and there you could see a squad of men running off out of range; now and then a man lying down, probably wounded or stunned, would rise and try to run, soon to tumble from the shots we sent after him. After the action I went all over the field of battle, visiting every part of it; but in no place was there anything like the number of dead upon the same space of ground as here in this little field. Our old fashioned guns, loaded as they were, and at such close quarters, had done fearful execution. This is undoubtedly the same field General Grant speaks of in the Century article, but he is mistaken when he speaks of the dead being from both sides. There were no Union dead in that field.

Our casualties were small. In our little set of college boys only one, was hurt; he receiving a wound in the leg, which caused its amputation. The bayonet of my gun was shot off, but possibly that was done by some man behind me, firing just as I threw the muzzle of my gun into his way. I didn't notice it until, in loading my gun, I struck my hand against the jagged end of the broken piece.

Defeat, Regrouping, and Counter-attacking

Late in the day, the Union lines finally broke and fell back to the landing. This is Olney's account of that retreat, and what took place on the second day of the battle.

The Confederates had all they wanted of charging across the field, and let us alone. But just to our left General Johnston had personally organized and started a heavy assaulting column. Overwhelmed by numbers, the Forty-first and Thirty-second Illinois gave way from the position they had so tenaciously held, but one of their last shots mortally wounded the Confederate general. The gallant Lieutenant-Colonel of the Forty-first, whom we had cheered as we moved out in the morning, was killed, and his regiment, broken and cut to pieces, did not renew the fight. Making that break in our line, after four or five hours of as hard fighting as ever occurred on this continent, was the turning point of the day. American had met American in fair, stand-up fight, and our side was beaten, because we could not reinforce the point which was assailed by the concentrated forces of the enemy.

Of course, the giving way on our left necessitated our abandoning the side of the field from whence we had annihilated an assaulting column. We moved back a short distance in the woods, and a crowd of our enemies promptly occupied the position we had left. Then began the first real, prolonged fighting experienced by our regiment that day. Our success in crushing the first attack had exhilarated us. We had tasted blood and were thoroughly aroused. Screening ourselves behind every log and tree, all broken into squads, the enemy broken up likewise, we gave back shot for shot and yell for yell. The very madness of bloodthirstiness possessed us. To kill, to exterminate the beings in front of us was our whole desire. Such energy and force was too much for our enemies, and ere long we saw squads of them rising from the ground and running away. Again there was no foe in our front. Ammunition was getting short, but happily a wagon came up with cartridges, and we took advantage of the lull to fill our boxes. We had not yet lost many men and were full of fight.

This contest exploded all my notions derived from histories and pictures, of the way men stand up in the presence of the enemy. Unless in making an assault or moving forward, both sides hugged the ground as closely as they possibly could and still handle their guns. I doubt if a human being could have existed three minutes, if standing erect in open ground under such a fire as we here experienced. As for myself, at the beginning I jumped behind a little sapling not more than six inches in diameter, and instantly about six men ranged themselves behind me, one behind the other. I thought they would certainly shoot my ears off, and I would be in luck if the side of my head didn't go. The reports of their guns were deafening. A savage remonstrance was unheeded. I was behind a sapling and proposed to stay there. They were behind me and proposed to stay there.

The sapling did me a good turn, small as it was. It caught some Rebel bullets, as I ascertained for a certainty afterwards. I fancied at the time that I heard the spat of the bullets as they struck.

Here my particular chum was wounded by a spent ball, and crawled off the field. I can see him yet, writhing at my feet, grasping the leaves and sticks in the horrible pain which the blow from a spent ball inflicts. A bullet struck the top of the forehead of the wit of the company, plowing along the skull without breaking it. His dazed expression, as he turned instinctively to crawl to the rear, was so comical as to cause a laugh even there.

The lull caused by the death of General Johnston did not last long, and again on our left flank great masses of the enemy appeared, and we had to fall back two or three hundred yards.

Then began another fight. But this time the odds were overwhelmingly against us. At it we went, but in front and quartering on the left thick masses of the enemy slowly but steadily advanced upon us. This time it was a log I got behind, kneeling, loading and firing into the dense ranks of the enemy advancing right in front, eager to kill, kill! I lost thought of companions, until a ball struck me fair in the side, just under the arm, knocking me over. I felt it go clear through my body, struggled on the ground with the effect of the blow for an instant, recovered myself, sprang to my feet, saw I was alone, my comrades already on the run, the enemy close in on the left as well as front — saw it all at a glance, felt I was mortally wounded, and — took to my heels. Run! such time was never made before; overhauled my companions in no time; passed them; began to wonder that a man shot through the body could run so fast, and to suspect that perhaps I was not mortally wounded after all; felt for the hole the ball had made, found it in the blouse and shirt, bad bruise on the ribs, nothing more — spent ball; never relaxed my speed; saw everything around — see it yet. I see the enemy close in on the flank, pouring in their fire at short range. I see our men running for their lives, men every instant tumbling forward limp on their faces, men falling wounded and rolling on the ground, the falling bullets raising little puffs of dust on apparently every foot of ground, a bullet through my hair, a bullet through my trousers. I hear the cruel *iz, iz,* of the minie balls everywhere. Ahead I see artillery galloping for the landing, and crowds of men running with almost equal speed, and all in the same direction. I even see the purple tinge given by the setting sun to the dust and smoke of battle. I see unutterable defeat, the success of the rebellion, a great catastrophe, a moral and physical cataclysm.

No doubt, in less time than it takes to recall these impressions, we ran out of this horrible gauntlet — a party who shall be nameless still in the lead of the regiment.

Before getting out of it we crossed our camp ground, and here one of our college set, the captain of the company fell, with several holes through his body, while two others of our set were wounded. In that short race at least one-third of our little command were stricken down.

Immediately behind us the Confederates closed in, and the brave General Prentiss and the gallant remains of his command were cut off and surrendered. As we passed out of range of the enemy's fire we mingled with the masses of troops skurrying towards the landing, all semblance of organization lost. It was a great crowd of beaten troops. Pell-mell we rushed towards the landing. As we approached it we saw a row of siege guns, manned and ready for action, while a dense mass of unorganized infantry were rallied to their support. No doubt they were men from every regiment on the field, rallied by brave officers for the last and final stand.

We passed them—or, at least, I did. As I reached the top of the bluff I saw, marching up, in well dressed lines, the advance of General Nelson's division of Buell's army, then being ferried across the river. They moved up the bluff and took part in repulsing the last, rather feeble assault made at dark by a small portion of the enemy, though the main defense was made by brave men collected from every quarter of the field, determined to fight to the last.

As for myself, I was alone in the crowd. My regiment was thoroughly scattered. I was considerably hurt and demoralized, and didn't take a hand in the last repulse of the enemy. Darkness came on, and then, for the first time since morning, the horrid din of fire-arms ceased. An examination showed that the ball, though it had hit me fair on the rib, was so far spent that it only made a bad bruise and respiration painful. A requisition on the sugar and hard tack followed, and then, as I happened to be near an old house filled with wounded, most of the night was spent in carrying them water.

Every fifteen minutes the horizon was lighted up by the flash of a great gun from one of our gunboats, as it sent a shell over towards the Confederate bivouacs in the woods. General Lew Wallace's division at last reached the battle field, and was placed by General Grant on the right, preparatory to renewing the fight in the morning. All night long the fresh divisions of Buell's army were being ferried across the river, and placed in position. A light rain came on, putting out the fires kindled by the battle.

The next morning the contest was begun by Wallace's division of Buell's army. The remnants of Grant's army that had any fight left in them, slowly collected together on the right.

My own regiment, when I found its colors, had as many men together, probably, as any in Hurlbut's division, but there could not have been more than one hundred and fifty. It was the same, I suspect, with every regiment that had been hotly engaged. The men were thoroughly scattered. Soldiers of pluck joined us who could not find their own command, and no doubt some of ours joined other regiments.

When our general was again about to lead our division to the front, I was only too glad to avail myself of permission to join a body of men to support a battery in reserve. Badly bruised, sore and worn out, I sat or lay on the ground near the guns, while Monday's battle progressed, the sound of it getting farther and farther away. About two o'clock we saw the cavalry moving to the front, and knew the enemy had retreated.

That night, as we collected on our old camp ground, what eager inquiries were made! With what welcome did we greet each new arrival; how excitedly the events of the last two days were discussed! We found that from the fourteen in our tent, one was killed, one mortally wounded, and seven others more or less severely wounded, only five escaping unhurt. This proportion, of course, was very unusual. The regiment itself, which had not lost many in the first two fights we made, was still, on account of the disastrous retreat under a flank fire, one of the heaviest losers, in proportion to the numbers engaged, in the whole army.

The feeling in the army after the battle was very bitter. All felt that even a few hours' notice of the impending attack, spent in preparation to receive it, would have been ample to have enabled us to give the Confederates such a reception as Beauregard feared and expected, and to have defeated them. It was long before General Grant regained the confidence of the army and country that he lost that day. He and Sherman here learned a lesson that they never forgot, but they learned it at fearful cost to the country and to us.

...

The thousands of youthful dead left on that bloody battlefield demonstrated that we have a country and a race worthy to take the lead in the march of human advancement.

CHAPTER FIVE

*SHELLS WHISTLED AROUND ME BUT MY BALLOON
AND I ESCAPED*

— THE CIVIL WAR "AIR-FORCES" —

*O*n June 16, 1861, across the street from the White House, a curious spectacle was taking place. A large hydrogen gas balloon, piloted by Thaddeus S. C. Lowe, floated about 500 feet above Washington D.C. From this lofty eminence, Mr. Lowe used a telegraph line that ran from his balloon to the White House to send this message:

"To President United States:

This point of observation commands an area nearly fifty miles in diameter. The city with its girdle of encampments presents a superb scene. I have pleasure in sending you this first dispatch ever telegraphed from an aerial station and in acknowledging indebtedness to your encouragement for the opportunity of demonstrating the availability of the science of aeronautics in the service of the country.

-T.S.C. Lowe."

Lowe had arranged the demonstration to impress President Lincoln with the fact that a Balloon Corps could be very useful to the Union Army. Of course, he also wanted to make sure that he would be in command of any such Corps. He soon got his wish when he was named *Chief Aeronaut of the brand new Union Army Balloon Corps.*

During its existence, Lowe's Corps would use six different balloons to take over 3,000 flights to make maps, observe the enemy, and provide live battle reports; but Lowe's balloons were not the only ones in the air during the war.

The Confederate Army sent balloons aloft to watch McClellan's Army during his Peninsular Campaign of 1862. The first was a hot air balloon under the command of Captain John R. Bryan. After a handful of flights, this balloon was not used again.

However, a new gas balloon under the command of E. P. Alexander took its place and was used throughout the defense of Richmond, and another flew over the city until the summer of 1863.

At the Battle of Seven Pines (May 31, 1862), both Alexander and Lowe were aloft giving their commanders live reports of the battle. This was the first time that balloons were used to give Army commanders live reports of a battle's progress from the air.

Both Alexander and Lowe also made flights from boats on the rivers near the Armies. Making the USS George Washington Parke Custis the first aircraft carrier, and the CSS Teaser the second.

In April 1863, Lowe's Balloon Corps was disbanded because of political disputes within the Army, and the Confederates never fielded another balloon after the one over Richmond was lost in the summer of 1863. So, the Civil War "Air Forces" came to an end, but the men who went up in the balloons came away with some great stories to tell...

A General Set Adrift

All balloon flights made during the Civil War were "tethered" flights, meaning that the balloon was tied to the ground with large ropes. This was done because the pilot had no control of where a *balloon went when in free flight. The balloon was at the mercy of the wind, and it would have been possible to be blown deep into enemy territory and captured if the balloons were not tethered.*

That does not mean that there were never any accidental free flights, as this story[8] from war correspondent George Alfred Townsend clearly demonstrates.

General Fitz John Porter.

On the 11th of April, at five o'clock, an event at once amusing and thrilling occurred at our quarters. The commander-in-chief had appointed his personal and confidential friend, General Fitz John Porter, to conduct the siege of Yorktown. Porter was a polite, soldierly gentleman, and a native of New Hampshire, who had been in the regular army since early manhood. He fought gallantly in the Mexican war, being thrice promoted and once seriously wounded, and he was now forty years of age, — handsome, enthusiastic, ambitious, and popular. He made frequent ascensions with Lowe, and learned to go aloft alone. One day he ascended thrice, and finally seemed as cosily at home in the firmament as upon the solid earth. It is needless to say that he grew careless, and on this particular morning leaped into the car and demanded the cables to be let out with all speed. I saw with some surprise that the flurried assistants were sending up the great straining canvas with a single rope attached. The enormous bag was only partially inflated, and the loose folds opened and shut with a

---

[8] Taken from *Campaigns of a Non-Combatant, and His Romaunt Abroad During The War*, by George Alfred Townsend, 1866.

crack like that of a musket. Noisily, fitfully, the yellow mass rose into the sky, the basket rocking like a feather in the zephyr; and just as I turned aside to speak to a comrade, a sound came from overhead, like the explosion of a shell, and something striking me across the face laid me flat upon the ground.

Half blind and stunned, I staggered to my feet, but the air seemed full of cries and curses. Opening my eyes ruefully, I saw all faces turned upwards, and when I looked above, — the balloon was adrift.

The treacherous cable, rotted with vitriol, had snapped in twain; one fragment had been the cause of my downfall, and the other trailed, like a great entrail, from the receding car, where Fitz John Porter was bounding upward upon a Pegasus that he could neither check nor direct.

The whole army was agitated by the unwonted occurrence. From battery No. 1, on the brink of the York, to the mouth of Warwick River, every soldier and officer was absorbed. Far within the Confederate lines the confusion extended. We heard the enemy's alarm-guns, and directly the signal flags were waving up and down our front.

The General appeared directly over the edge of the car. He was tossing his hands frightenedly, and shouting something that we could not comprehend.

"O—pen—the—valve!" called Lowe, in his shrill tones; "climb—to—the—netting—and—reach—the—valve—rope."

"The valve!—the valve!" repeated a multitude of tongues, and all gazed with thrilling interest at the retreating hulk that still kept straight upward, swerving neither to the east nor the west.

It was a weird spectacle,—that frail, fading oval, gliding against the sky, floating in the serene azure, the little vessel swinging silently beneath, and a hundred thousand martial men watching the loss of their brother in arms, but powerless to relieve or recover him. Had Fitz John Porter been drifting down the rapids of Niagara, he could not have been so far from human assistance. But we saw him directly, no bigger than a child's toy, clambering up the netting and reaching for the cord.

"He can't do it," muttered a man beside me; "the wind blows the valve-rope to and fro, and only a spry, cool-headed fellow can catch it."

We saw the General descend, and appearing again over the edge of the basket, he seemed to be motioning to the breathless hordes below, the story of his failure. Then he dropped out of sight, and when we next saw him, he was reconnoitring the Confederate works through a long black spy-glass. A great laugh went up and down the lines as this cool procedure was observed, and then a cheer of applause ran from group to group. For a moment it was doubtful that the balloon would float in either direction; it seemed to falter, like an irresolute being, and moved reluctantly southeastward, towards Fortress Monroe. A huzza, half uttered, quivered on every lip. All eyes glistened, and some were dim with tears of joy. But the wayward canvas now turned due westward, and was blown rapidly toward the Confederate works. Its course was fitfully direct, and the wind seemed to veer often, as if contrary currents, conscious of the opportunity, were struggling for the possession of the daring navigator. The south wind held mastery for awhile, and the balloon passed the Federal front amid a howl of despair from the soldiery. It kept right on, over sharpshooters, rifle-pits, and outworks, and finally passed, as if to deliver up its freight, directly over the heights of Yorktown. The cool courage, either of heroism or despair, had seized upon Fitz John Porter. He turned his black glass upon the ramparts and masked cannon below, upon the remote camps, upon the beleaguered town, upon the guns of Gloucester Point, and upon distant Norfolk. Had he been reconnoitring from a secure perch at the tip of the moon, he could not have been more vigilant, and the Confederates probably thought this some Yankee device to peer into their sanctuary in despite of ball or shell. None of their great guns could be brought to bear upon the balloon; but there were some discharges of musketry that appeared to have no effect, and finally even these demonstrations ceased. Both armies in solemn silence were gazing aloft, while the imperturbable mariner continued to spy out the land.

The sun was now rising behind us, and roseate rays struggled up to the zenith, like the arcs made by showery bombs. They threw a hazy atmosphere upon the balloon, and the light shone through the network like the sun through the ribs of the skeleton ship in the Ancient Mariner. Then, as all looked agape, the air-craft "plunged, and tacked, and veered," and drifted rapidly toward the Federal lines again.

The allelujah that now went up shook the spheres, and when he had regained our camp limits, the General was seen clambering up again to clutch the valve-rope. This time he was successful, and the balloon fell like a stone, so that all hearts once more leaped up, and the cheers were hushed. Cavalry rode pell-mell from several directions, to reach the place of descent, and the General's personal staff galloped past me like the wind, to be the first at his debarkation. I followed the throng of soldiery with due haste, and came up to the horsemen in a few minutes. The balloon had struck a canvas tent with great violence, felling it as by a bolt, and the General, unharmed, had disentangled himself from innumerable folds of oiled canvas, and was now the cynosure of an immense group of people. While the officers shook his hands, the rabble bawled their satisfaction in hurrahs, and a band of music marching up directly, the throng on foot and horse gave him a vociferous escort to his quarters.

Anti-Aircraft Fire

On another instance, Mr. Townsend went aloft with Thaddeus Lowe, but he was soon afraid that his balloon would never make it back to earth...

"Stand by your cables," he said, and the bags of ballast were at once cut away. Twelve men took each a rope in hand, and played out slowly, letting us glide gently upward. The earth seemed to be falling away, and we poised motionless in the blue ether. The

George Alfred Townsend, in 1899.

tree-tops sank downward, the hills dropped noiselessly through space, and directly the Chickahominy was visible beyond us, winding like a ribbon of silver through the ridgy landscape.

...

A panorama so beautiful would have been rare at any time, but this was thrice interesting from its past and coming associations. Across those plains the hordes at our feet were either to advance victoriously, or be driven eastward with dusty banners and dripping hands. Those white farm-houses were to be receptacles for the groaning and the mangled; thousands were to be received beneath the turf of those pasture fields; and no rod of ground on any side, should not, sooner or later, smoke with the blood of the slain.

"Guess I got 'em now, jest where I want 'em," said Lowe, with a gratified laugh; "jest keep still as you mind to, and squint your eye through my glass, while I make a sketch of the roads and the country. Hold hard there, and anchor fast!" he screamed to the people below. Then he fell imperturbably to work, sweeping the country with his hawk-eye, and escaping nothing that could contribute to the completeness of his jotting.

We had been but a few minutes thus poised, when close below, from the edge of a timber stretch, puffed a volume of white smoke. A second afterward, the air quivered with the peal of a cannon. A third, and we heard the splitting shriek of a shell, that passed a little to our left, but in exact range, and burst beyond us in the ploughed field, heaving up the clay as it exploded.

"Ha!" said Lowe, "they have got us foul! Haul in the cables—quick!" he shouted, in a fierce tone.

At the same instant, the puff, the report, and the shriek were repeated; but this time the shell burst to our right in mid-air, and scattered fragments around and below us.

"Another shot will do our business," said Lowe, between his teeth; "it isn't a mile, and they have got the range."

Again the puff and the whizzing shock. I closed my eyes, and held my breath hard. The explosion was so close, that the pieces of shell seemed driven across my face, and my ears quivered with the sound. I looked at Lowe, to see if he was struck. He had sprung to his feet, and clutched the cordage frantically.

"Are you pulling in there, you men?" he bellowed, with a loud imprecation.

"Puff! bang! whiz-z-z-z! splutter!" broke a third shell, and my heart was wedged in my throat.

I saw at a glimpse the whole bright landscape again. I heard the voices of soldiers below, and saw them running across fields, fences, and ditches, to reach our anchorage. I saw some drummer-boys digging in the field beneath for one of the buried shells. I saw the waving of signal flags, the commotion through the camps,—officers galloping their horses, teamsters whipping their mules, regiments turning out, drums beaten, and batteries limbered up. I remarked, last of all, the site of the battery that alarmed us, and, by a strange sharpness of sight and sense, believed that I saw the gunners swabbing, ramming, and aiming the pieces.

"Puff! bang! whiz-z-z-z! splutter! crash!"

"Puff! bang! whiz-z-z-z! splutter! crash!"

"My God!" said Lowe, hissing the words slowly and terribly, "they have opened upon us from another battery!"

The scene seemed to dissolve. A cold dew broke from my forehead. I grew blind and deaf. I had fainted.

"Pitch some water in his face," said somebody. "He ain't used to it. Hallo! there he comes to."

I staggered to my feet. There must have been a thousand men about us. They were looking curiously at the aeronaut and me. The balloon lay fuming and struggling on the clods.

"Three cheers for the Union bal-loon!" called a little fellow at my side.

"Hip, hip—hoorooar! hoorooar! hoorooar!"

The Confederate Aeronaut

The first Confederate Aeronaut was Captain John R. Bryan. He had no previous experience, and he really had no idea what he was getting himself into. Not only that, he was destined to have experiences on par with those of Mr. Townsend and General Porter. Here is Captain Bryan's account[9] of his time as the lone Aeronaut of the Confederate Army...

General Johnston had brought down with him from Richmond what I believe to be the first balloon used for millitary service during the war. It was nothing but a big cotton bag, coated over so as to make it air-tight, and intended to be inflated with hot air, as gas was a thing not to be had in those days and in those places. After being on the Peninsula for some days, General Johnston wrote to General Magruder, requesting him to detail someone who was thoroughly acquainted with the country, and who was capable of forming a correct opinion as to the number and character of the troops in front of him, in order that he might be assigned to do duty with General Johnston. This order, coming from General Johnston's headquarters, passed through my hands, as I was chief clerk in Magruder' s Adjutant-General's office, and being young, and, I fear, of a dare-devil spirit, and supposing that an assignment to this duty would bring me prominently into notice, and probably offer some opportunity for distinguishing myself (for since childhood I had been thoroughly familiar with all that section of country, and felt myself competent as to the other requirements). I therefore at once asked that I might be detailed for this service.

---

[9] Taken from the *Southern Historical Society Papers, Volume XXXIII*, edited by R. A. Brock, 1905.

Major Henry Bryan, Magruder's Adjutant-General, strongly dissuaded me from the undertaking, but I was so bent on it that I went in person to General Magruder and asked for the detail, which, after some little persuasion on my part, was granted to me, although my friends told me that it was more than likely that I would get myself into hot water, and very possibly (in case I should go into the enemy's lines) that I would get shot for my pains. Nevertheless, I joyfully received my orders, and mounting my horse, rode gaily over to Lee's farm, where General Johnston was, to report myself for special service. On arriving there I handed my orders in to the proper officer, and reported for duty. Having a number of acquaintances around headquarters, I tried to find out for what purpose I was needed, or to what duty I would probably be assigned, but could get no information. All I could learn was from Colonel Rhett, Johnston's Adjutant-General, that the General would be out presently, and would himself tell me what he wanted me to do.

After a while I was called into General Johnston's tent, and the General, looking at me, and seeming surprised that I was only a boy (for I was just twenty-one years old), began to question me quite closely as to what experience I had had in military affairs, how long I had been with the army, whether I could distinguish one branch of service from another, and the like.

Having answered these questions to General Johnston's satisfaction, the latter laid a map of the Peninsula on the table before him, and began questioning me about the different roads and creeks and fording places, and other topographical matters on the Peninsula. Having shown myself sufficiently familiar with these matters, the General then turned to Colonel Rhett and remarked, 'I think Mr. Bryan will do very well. You will please assign him to the balloon service to make the reconnoisances, and instruct him as to what information we want, and the kind of report we desire from him.' On hearing this order I at once sprang to my feet, protesting that while I could ride a horse, and would gladly do anything in my power, that I had never even seen a balloon, and that I knew absolutely nothing about the management of it, and that if the General simply wanted some information as to the position of the enemy and their numbers at any given point, that I would very cheerfully go into the lines and get this information and return as speedily as possible and report. My words had, however, small effect upon the General. He told me very curtly and positively that I had been assigned to him for duty, and that he expected me to perform the duty to which I was assigned without any questions. He added that he had plenty of scouts already, and what he wanted was a man to go up in the balloon, and that I could now go and prepare myself to be in readiness when sent for. This was pretty hard, but as there was no sort of question about it, I could only make my bow and walk out with as brave an appearance as possible. Shortly afterwards I was fully instructed as to all the details; that there was a crew of men already in charge of the balloon, who understood the management of it, as to the inflating, letting it ascend and drawing it down again by means of the rope which was attached to it (which passed around a windlass), and I was also instructed in the signals that I should make when up in the balloon, by means of a wig-wag flag, to tell those below what was wanted, whether I wished to go fast or slow, up or down. I was also given such information as was at hand as to the supposed position of the enemy, and was instructed to carefully note where each different arm of the service (infantry, artilery, and cavelry) was located, and I was further told to make a memorandum or map of all that I saw while up in the balloon, so as to be able to give the best and most accurate account of all I saw when I returned — provided of course, that I returned at all.

The balloon party were located behind a large thicket of pine trees about a half mile back of the Confederate lines, with a view of allowing the balloon to reach a considerable elevation before it could be seen by the enemy, who would, of course, fire at it in the hope of destroying it. As I had seen some artillery service, I was quite well aware that after attaining a certain height the ordinary field cannon could not be trained to bear upon me, so that the danger zone was only between the time I appeared above the top of the trees and the time when I should have reached such an elevation that their guns could no longer be trained upon me. My ardor to go on special service had been much cooled at the bare thought of being suspended in mid air by what appeared to me as a mere thread under a hot-air balloon, with the chances pretty strong that it would be burst by the shrapnel or shells of the enemy, when 'down would come baby and all.' However, I determined to make best of a bad bargain, and went to the balloon camp to study the situation and my new duties. I was not left long in suspense, for the next day I received an order from General Johnston to make my first ascension. The balloon was anchored to a long rope, probably a half of a mile long, which was tied to a tree and then coiled in a great number of coils, sailor fashion, on the ground, and then passed around a windlass, and was finally attached to a number of cords coming down from the balloon. From this cone of cords hung a good sized hamper, or basket in which I was to stand or kneel and make my observations. It did not take a very long time (in fact, it was accomplished much too quickly for my liking) to fill the balloon with hot air, for a plentiful supply of pine knots and turpentine had been made (to create a great heat under a flue, the end of which opened into the balloon), so that very soon I was told that my aerial horse was ready for me to mount and ride away. Therefore, with note book and pencil in my pocket, and a heart beneath it beating very furiously (although of course I put on a brave front to those about me), I stepped into the basket and gave the signal to rise. At first the balloon was let off quite gradually, and I began to ascend slowly. 'This is not so bad' I thought, but the worst was yet to come.

Hardly, however, had I got above the tree tops and obtained a view of the enemy's line than I observed a great commotion among them, men running here and there, and in a very few minutes they had run out a battery. I saw the officer in charge elevate the gun and carefully sight it at me, and give the signal to fire. "Boom!" went the cannon, and the shell whistled by me in most unpleasant proximity. For some minutes shells and bullets from the schrapnels (which burst in front of me) whistled and sang around me with a most unpleasant music; but my balloon and I escaped. As you may readily imagine, I did not feel very happy or comfortable; on the contrary, I was scared nearly breathless, and was exceedingly nervous. I at once gave the signal, 'faster,' and the balloon went upward more rapidly, and before long I reached an elevation above the line of fire, when I again signalled them to stop, and squatting down in the hamper, I tried to collect my thoughts and breathe more freely. I now began to recover my composure, when a most horrid thought intruded itself upon me. 'Whatever goes up is bound to come down,' is a trite, but a sad, true saying. I knew well I could not remain in this security forever; in fact, every moment that passed the hot air in my balloon became cooler. I therefore set to work. From my elevated position I could see the whole country in every direction. A wonderful panorama spread out beneath me. Chesapeake Bay, the York and the James rivers, Old Point Comfort and Hampton, and the fleets lying in both the York and the James, and the two opposing armies lying facing each other. I therefore took out my note-book and made a rough diagram showing the rivers, the roads and creeks, and marking where the different bodies of the enemy's troops were upon this little map, using the initial 'I' for infantry, 'C' for cavalry, 'A' for artillery, and 'W' for wagon trains, and I marked down about the number of troops that I estimated at each point. Now, this was not such an easy thing to do, as we may at first suppose, for the various currents of air made my balloon spin and revolve like a top (only very much slower), so that I must needs wait for a whole revolution to occur before I completed my sketch of any particular spot. Finally I gave the signal to lower the balloon, but hardly had I begun the descent when I saw that the enemy had prepared to give me a very warm reception as soon as I came within range, for they had run out a number of other batteries, and stood by their guns preparing for firing and aiming them at the spot I must pass on my way to terra firma. I therefore gave the signal, 'faster — faster,' and the men at the windlass put forth their best efforts, working in relays, and as fast as they could. However, it seemed all too slow to me, for I was soon again in the danger zone, and the enemy's guns opened on me, firing this time by batteries, four and six at a time, and filling the air with shells and bullets, and how I escaped I do not know, for some of their shells passed very close to me.

However, after what seemed to me an age, the balloon was finally wound down, and I stepped out of my basket once more upon Mother Earth. Mounting my horse I rode to General Johnston's headquarters to make my report. The General listened intently to what I told him, and asked very particularly as to the position of the different branches of the service, and as to their numbers, and spreading out his map on the table, made me show him where the different bodies of troops, artillery, and so on, were posted. When I had finished my report the General complimented me by saying I had done very well indeed. Therefore, at leaving I felt that my experiences were a thing of the past, and requested the General to assign me to the same duties which I had performed before I had joined him.

'My dear sir,' replied the General, 'I fear you forget that you are the only experienced aeronaut that I have with my army, and you will please hold yourself in readiness, as we may wish you to make another ascension at any time!' I felt complimented, but I was not elated.

That evening the whole balloon force was ordered to move to another point, somewhere nearer Yorktown, as the General did not think it safe that the balloons should go up from the same place again. Also, arrangement was made for increasing the speed in hauling down the balloon. This was that six artillery horses were hitched to the end of the rope which passed through the windlass, and upon the signal to lower the balloon they were ridden up the road and at full gallop, which brought the balloon down much more quickly. In a day or two a second ascent was made, at the General's orders, which was much like the first one, but with somewhat less trepidation by General Johnston's 'only experienced aeronaut,' who had already been nicknamed by his fellow soldiers 'Balloon Bryan,' and who was suspected by them of having a screw loose somewhere on account of his mad trips in the air, General Johnston received the second report about as he did the first, but still refused to discharge me from the balloon service, but ordered me to hold myself in readiness.

A few nights later I made another, and, I am glad to say, my last ascension, which came near being my last trip in anything; but I shall proceed to narrate that occurrence.

One night, just before the body fell back from Yorktown and fought the battle of Williamsburg (which was the 5th of May, 1862), the balloon squad was waked up one night with orders from General Johnston to fire up the balloon and make a reconnoisance as soon as possible. The courier who brought the order informed me privately that information had been received at headquarters from some of the scouts that the enemy was in motion and that General Johnston was very anxious to ascertain in what direction the move was to be made, and whether their troops were advancing upon more than one point. It was at this time near the full moon and the nights were as bright, almost as day. As soon, therefore, as the balloon was inflated I jumped into my basket, feeling quite at ease, as I had already made two ascensions, and as this was to be a night trip, I had but little fear of discovery and of being fired on, especially as the enemy were now in motion, and when marching could not so well arrange for this artillery service. But there was a still greater danger upon which I had never calculated. The Confederate troops, almost to a man, had never seen a balloon, and each time that I went up they

crowded around the balloon squad to watch this novel performance, and amused themselves by making many and varied
remarks, which were not very complimentary upon the whole
business and myself in particular. On this occasion the balloon, shining in the bright firelight, attracted a larger crowd
than usual, and the crew in charge had great difficulty in keeping them back out of their way, so they could properly perform their work. I therefore entered the basket and gave the
signal to rise, feeling, as I have said, unusually comfortable,
and I had ascended about two hundred feet when, all at once,
without any warning, the balloon was jerked upward as if by
some great force for about two miles, so it seemed to me. I
was breathless and gasping, and trembling like a leaf from fear
without knowing what had happened beyond the surmise that
the rope which held me to the earth had broken. What had
actually occurred I afterwards found was this: One of the soldiers who was drawn by curiosity to see the balloon ascend
had crowded, with the others, too near, and had unwittingly
stepped into the coil of rope, one end of which was attached to
the balloon, which, before he could step out again, tightened
around his leg and began pulling him up to the windlass,
whereupon he screamed loudly, and one of his friends seized
an axe and cut the rope, releasing him, but also releasing me.
Now, there I was, feeling as if I was a couple of miles up in the
air, absolutely helpless, with no idea of how to manage my
runaway steed, and with every prospect that I would eventually very reluctantly land in the enemy's lines, which meant a
long term of imprisonment, or else that my balloon would
come down in the Chesapeake Bay, with no means of my regaining the shore, which perhaps meant being drowned, but
which I much preferred to the former. These thoughts were

not of a very consoling nature. One thing I knew was that when the heat died out of the balloon I must make a graceful descent; but as to where I should land I could not even guess. To say that I was frightened but faintly expresses it, for the almost instantaneous ascent I had made had not only taken all the breath out of my body, but seemed also to have deprived me of all my nerve and courage for the time being. However, after a while I recovered my breath and found, upon careful examination, that my heart was beating much as usual. The balloon had now reached its equilibrium, and was apparently standing quietly (for there was little air stirring) over the Confederate army, and I was looking down to where, far below me, lay the York River and the surrounding country which I knew so well.

I was not long left to enjoy the beauties of this scene, for the wind freshened up, and, to my utmost dismay, I found myself being blown from the Confederate lines over into those of the enemy. It is impossible to describe my feelings. I felt that I was not only leaving my home and friends forever, but was slowly drifting to certain capture. Imagine, therefore, my great delight when, after drifting along for some distance, the wind veered and I was blown back toward the Confederate lines. (This ascension had been made from a point back of Dam No. 2, i. e., Wynn's Mill, on the Confederate lines.) It was evident that the balloon was cooling and settling, so that I was getting nearer and nearer to the earth. This was in many respects a great comfort, but it was not unalloyed with new dangers. As I have said, the balloon having now drawn near the earth (a few hundred feet above it I suppose) I was blown from the enemy's lines over the Confederate army, but, alas! in a far different locality from where I had ascended. Therefore, when my balloon passed over the spot where Col. Ward's Second Florida Regiment was encamped, they turned out en masse, and believing me to be a Yankee spy, followed me on foot, firing at me as fast as they could. In vain I cried to them that I was a good Confederate; the only answer I received was from the whistling of their bullets. I was as a thing haunted, and knew not which way to turn. However, the wind freshened again, and I was blown out over York River, which, although half a mile wide at Yorktown, is three or four miles wide where I was now suspended in the air. The balloon began now to settle quite rapidly, and it was evident that I would be dumped unceremoniously in the middle of this broad expanse of water.

I, therefore, began to undress, preparatory to my long swim, but I regret to record that being a young man I was what is termed 'somewhat dressy,' and I had on a pair of very tight fitting boots, which, do what I might, I found impossible to pull off, and after tugging and scuffling in every conceivable position that my cramped quarters in the basket would permit, and still being unable to rid myself of those accursed boots (which were not long since my joy and pride.) I fortunately remembered my pocket knife, and had soon ripped them down the back and joyfully dropped them over the edge of my basket. The balloon was now so near the river that I could hear my rope splashing in the water as it dragged along over the surface and I was waiting to begin my swim at any moment when the wind again changed and blew me towards the Williamsburg shore. This was, indeed, luck of the greatest kind. After travelling a short distance inland, my balloon, by this time having settled nearly to the ground, I slipped over the side of the basket and sliding down the rope safely, joyfully stood once more on my native heath. I had landed in an orchard, and running with my rope, as the balloon passed over an apple tree, I twisted it quickly about the tree trunk, and after a few ineffectual flops, my balloon sank, exhausted to the ground. What remains to be told can be related in a few words.

I dressed myself as quickly as possible and made my way to a neighboring farm house, where, after quite a hot discussion with the farmer, I succeeded in securing a horse and rode back to General Johnston's Headquarters, a distance of about eight miles, and made my report as to my experience and as to what I had seen. On this trip my balloon had (so far as I can judge) made a half moon circuit of about fifteen miles, about four miles of which was over York River. As to the height to which I attained I cannot well compute.

The information which I was able to give General Johnston as to the roads upon which the enemy were now moving, enabled him to prepare for an attack which was made by them early the next morning just before day.

I was among those who awaited the approach of the enemy, and you will pardon me if I say that it gave me no little satisfaction to aim my rifle at those who had so recently and so frequently taken a wing shot at me.

CHAPTER SIX

OUR AMMUNITION WAS ENTIRELY EXHAUSTED

— PHILIP HENRY SHERIDAN —

*P*hilip Sheridan cut a somewhat odd figure as a General in the Union Army. He was regularly referred to by the nickname "Little Phil" due to his small stature (he was just 5' 5" tall); and President Lincoln once described him like this, "A brown, chunky little chap, with a long body, short legs, not enough neck to hang him, and such long arms that if his ankles itch he can scratch them without stooping."

Appearance notwithstanding, Sheridan proved his worth on the battlefield. After his first experience commanding troops in combat at the Battle of Booneville (Mississippi), his commanding officers were so impressed with him that they recommended him for promotion to Brigadier General. The recommendation ended with the following statement, "The undersigned respectfully beg that you will obtain the promotion of Sheridan. He is worth his weight in gold."

From Booneville to Appomattox, Sheridan commanded well; and by the end of the war he was regarded as a hero throughout the North. Here are some stories[10] from his time in command...

---

[10] Taken from the *Personal Memoirs of P. H. Sheridan,* by Phillip Henry Sheridan, 1888.

Foraging Party Makes a Surprising Discovery

While commanding troops in Tennessee, Sheridan faced the dilemma of how to supply his men and horses in hostile territory. The answer was of course "foraging." Little did he know, one of his foraging parties was destined to make an interesting discovery...

I employed a brigade about once a week in the duty of collecting and bringing in forage, sending out sometimes as many as a hundred and fifty wagons to haul the grain which my scouts had previously located. In nearly every one of these expeditions the enemy was encountered, and the wagons were usually loaded while the skirmishers kept up a running fire, Often there would occur a respectable brush, with the loss on each side of a number of killed and wounded. The officer in direct command always reported to me personally whatever had happened during the time he was out—the result of his reconnoissance, so to speak, for that was the real nature of these excursions—and on one occasion the colonel in command, Colonel Conrad, of the Fifteenth Missouri, informed me that he got through without much difficulty; in fact, that everything had gone all right and been eminently satisfactory, except that in returning he had been mortified greatly by the conduct of the two females belonging to the detachment and division train at my headquarters. These women, he said, had given much annoyance by getting drunk, and to some extent demoralizing his men. To say that I was astonished at his statement would be a mild way of putting it, and had I not known him to be a most upright man and of sound sense, I should have doubted not only his veracity, but his sanity. Inquiring who they were and for further details, I was informed that there certainly were in the command two females, that in some mysterious manner had attached themselves to the service as soldiers; that one, an East Tennessee woman, was a teamster in the division wagon-train and the other a private soldier in a cavalry company temporarily attached to my headquarters for escort duty. While out on the foraging expedition these Amazons had secured a supply of "apple-jack" by some means, got very drunk, and on the return had fallen into Stone River and been nearly drowned. After they had been fished from the water, in the process of resuscitation their sex was disclosed, though up to this time it appeared to be known only to each other. The story was straight and the circumstance clear, so, convinced of Conrad's continued sanity, I directed the provost-marshal to bring in arrest to my headquarters the two disturbers of Conrad's peace of mind. After some little search the East Tennessee woman was found in camp, somewhat the worse for the experiences of the day before, but awaiting her fate content idly smoking a cob-pipe. She was brought to me, and put in duress under charge of the division surgeon until her companion could be secured. To the doctor she related that the year before she had "refugeed" from East Tennessee, and on arriving in Louisville assumed men's apparel and sought and obtained employment as a teamster in the quartermaster's department. Her features were very large, and so coarse and masculine was her general appearance that she would readily have passed as a man, and in her case the deception was no doubt easily practiced. Next day the "she dragoon" was caught, and proved to be a rather prepossessing young woman, and though necessarily bronzed and hardened by exposure, I doubt if, even with these marks of campaigning, she could have deceived as readily as did her companion.

How the two got acquainted, I never learned, and though they had joined the army independently of each other, yet an intimacy had sprung up between them long before the mishaps of the foraging expedition. They both were forwarded to army headquarters, and, when provided with clothing suited to their sex, sent back to Nashville, and thence beyond our lines to Louisville.

The Battle of Stones River

General Phillip Henry Sheridan.

At the Battle of Stones River (December 31, 1862 - January 2, 1863), Sheridan and his division faced the brunt of a fierce Confederate assault. They held their position until they ran out of ammunition and were forced to withdraw. This is General Sheridan's account of the battle...

During the evening *[December 30]*, feeling keenly all the solicitude which attends one in anticipation of a battle, I examined my position with great care, inspecting its whole length several times to remedy any defects that might exist, and to let the men see that I was alive to their interests and advantages. After dark, I went back to the rear of my reserve brigade, and establishing my headquarters behind the trunk of a large fallen tree, which would shelter me somewhat from the cold December wind, lay down beside a small campfire to get some rest.

...

Long before dawn my division breakfasted, and was assembled under arms, the infantry in line, the cannoneers at their pieces, but while we were thus preparing, all the recent signs of activity in the enemy's camp were hushed, a death-like stillness prevailing in the cedars to our front. Shortly after daylight *[Confederate]* General Hardee opened the engagement, just as *[General]* Sill had predicted, by a fierce attack on *[General]* Johnson's division, the extreme right of the Union line. Immediate success attending this assault, Hardee extended the attack gradually along in front of *[General]* Davis, his movement taking the form of a wheel to the right, the pivot being nearly opposite the left of my division. Johnson's division soon gave way, and two of Davis's brigades were forced to fall back with it, though stubbornly resisting the determined and sweeping onset.

In the meantime the enemy had also attacked me, advancing across an old cotton-field in Sill's front in heavy masses, which were furiously opened upon by Bush's battery from Sill's line, and by Hescock's and Houghtaling's batteries, which had an oblique fire on the field from a commanding position in rear of my centre. The effect of this fire on the advancing column was terrible, but it continued on till it reached the edge of the timber where Sill's right lay, when my infantry opened at a range of not over fifty yards. For a short time the Confederates withstood the fire, but then wavered, broke, and fell back toward their original line. As they retired, Sill's brigade followed in a spirited charge, driving them back across the open ground and behind their intrenchments. In this charge the gallant Sill was killed; a rifle ball passing through his upper lip and penetrating the brain. Although this was a heavy loss, yet the enemy's discomfiture was such as to give us an hour's time, and as Colonel Greusel, Thirty-sixth Illinois, succeeded to Sill's command, I directed him, as he took charge, to recall the brigade to its original position, for the turning-column on my extreme right was now assuming the most menacing attitude, and it was urgently necessary to prepare for it.

When that portion of the enemy driven back by Sill recovered from its repulse it again advanced to the attack, this time directing its efforts chiefly upon my extreme right, and the front of Woodruff's brigade of Davis's division, which brigade still held on in its first position. In front of my centre the Confederates were again driven back, but as the assault on Woodruff was in conjunction with an advance of the column that had forced Johnson to retire, Woodruff was compelled unfortunately to give way, and two regiments on the right of my line went with him, till they rallied on the two reserve regiments which, in anticipation of the enemy's initiatory attack I had sent to Sill's rear before daylight.

Both Johnson's and Davis's divisions were now practically gone from our line, having retired with a loss of all formation, and they were being closely pursued by the enemy, whose columns were following the arc of a circle that would ultimately carry him in on my rear. In consequence of the fact that this state of things would soon subject me to a fire in reverse, I hastily withdrew Sill's brigade and the reserve regiments supporting it, and ordered Roberts's brigade, which at the close of the enemy's second repulse had changed front toward the south and formed in column of regiments, to cover the withdrawal by a charge on the Confederates as they came into the timber where my right had originally rested. Roberts made the charge at the proper time, and was successful in checking the enemy's advance, thus giving us a breathing-spell, during which I was able to take up a new position with Schaefer's and Sill's brigades on the commanding ground to the rear, where Hescock's and Houghtaling's batteries had been posted all the morning.

The general course of this new position was at right angles with my original line, and it took the shape of an obtuse angle, with my three batteries at the apex. Davis, and Carlin of his division, endeavored to rally their men here on my right, but their efforts were practically unavailing,—though the calm and cool appearance of Carlin, who at the time was smoking a stumpy pipe, had some effect, and was in strong contrast to the excited manner of Davis, who seemed overpowered by the disaster that had befallen his command. But few could be rallied, however, as the men were badly demoralized, and most of them fell back beyond the Wilkinson pike, where they reorganized behind the troops of General Thomas.

At this juncture the enemy's turning-column began advancing again in concert with *[Confederate General]* Cheatham's division, and as the extreme left of the Confederates was directed on Griscom's house, and their right on the Blanton house, my new position was in danger of envelopment.

...

I had hardly got straightened out in this last place when I was attacked by Cheatham's division, which, notwithstanding the staggering blows it had previously received from Sill and Roberts, now again moved forward in conjunction with the wheeling movement under the immediate command of Hardee. One of the most sanguinary contests of the day now took place. In fulfillment of *[Confederate Commanding General]* Bragg's original design no doubt, Cheatham's division attacked on my left, while heavy masses under Hardee, covered by batteries posted on the high ground formerly occupied by my guns, assaulted my right, the whole force advancing simultaneously. At the same time the enemy opened an artillery fire from his intrenchments in front of Murfreesboro', and it seemed that he was present on every side. My position was strong, however, located in the edge of a dense cedar thicket and commanding a slight depression of open ground that lay in my front. My men were in good spirits too, notwithstanding they had been a good deal hustled around since daylight, with losses that had told considerably on their numbers. Only a short distance now separated the contending lines, and as the batteries on each side were not much more than two hundred yards apart when the enemy made his assault, the artillery fire was fearful in its effect on the ranks of both contestants, the enemy's heavy masses staggering under the torrent of shell and canister from our batteries, while our lines were thinned by his ricochetting projectiles, that rebounded again and again over the thinly covered limestone formation and sped on to the rear of Negley. But all his efforts to dislodge or destroy us were futile, and for the first time since daylight General Hardee was seriously checked in the turning movement he had begun for the purpose of getting possession of the Nashville pike, and though reinforced until two-fifths of Bragg's army was now at his command, yet he met with repulse after repulse, which created great gaps in his lines and taught him that to overwhelm us was hopeless.

As the enemy was recoiling from his first attack, I received a message from *[Union Commanding General]* Rosecrans telling me that he was making new dispositions, and directing me to hold on where I was until they were completed. From this I judged that the existing conditions of the battle would probably require a sacrifice of my command, so I informed Roberts and Schaefer that we must be prepared to meet the demand on us by withstanding the assault of the enemy, no matter what the outcome. Every energy was therefore bent to the simple holding of our ground, and as ammunition was getting scarce, instructions were given throughout the command to have it reserve its fire till the most effective moment. In a little while came a second and a third assault, and although they were as daring and furious as the first, yet in each case the Confederates were repulsed, driven back in confusion, but not without deadly loss to us, for the noble Roberts was killed, and Colonel Harrington, of the Twenty-Seventh Illinois, who succeeded to his brigade, was mortally wounded a few minutes later. I had now on the death-roll three brigade commanders, and the loss of subordinate officers and men was appalling, but their sacrifice had accomplished the desired result; they had not fallen in vain. Indeed, the bravery and tenacity of my division gave to Rosecrans the time required to make new dispositions, and exacted from our foes the highest commendations.

A lull followed the third fierce assault, and an investigation showed that, with the exception of a few rounds in my brigade, our ammunition was entirely exhausted; and while it was apparent that the enemy was reluctant to renew the conflict in my front, yet I was satisfied I could not hold on much longer without the danger of ultimate capture, so I prepared to withdraw as soon as the troops of Rousseau's division, which had been ordered to take up a line on my right, came into position. Schaefer's and Sill's brigades being without a cartridge, I directed them to fix bayonets for a charge, and await any attempt of the enemy to embarrass my retreat, while Roberts's brigade, offering such resistance as its small quantity of ammunition would permit, was pulled slowly in toward the Nashville pike. Eighty of the horses of Houghtaling's battery having been killed, an attempt was made to bring his guns back by hand over the rocky ground, but it could not be done, and we had to abandon them. Hescock also had lost most of his horses, but all his guns were saved. Bush's battery lost two pieces, the tangled underbrush in the dense cedars proving an obstacle to getting them away which his almost superhuman exertions could not surmount. Thus far the bloody duel had cost me heavily, one-third of my division being killed or wounded. I had already three brigade commanders killed; a little later I lost my fourth—Colonel Schaefer.

...

Rosecrans, whom I now met in the open ground west of the railroad, behind Palmer, directed that my command should relieve Wood's division, which was required to fall back and take up the new line that had been marked out while I was holding on in the cedars. His usually florid face had lost its ruddy color, and his anxious eyes told that the disasters of the morning were testing his powers to the very verge of endurance, but he seemed fully to comprehend what had befallen us. His firmly set lips and, the calmness with which his instructions were delivered inspired confidence in all around him; and expressing approbation of what my division had done, while deliberately directing it to a new point, he renewed in us all the hope of final victory, though it must be admitted that at this phase of the battle the chances lay largely with the enemy.

...

I was ordered by Rosecrans to prepare to make a charge should the enemy again assault us. In anticipation of this work I massed my troops in close column. The expected attack never came, however, but the shot and shell of a furious cannonade told with fatal effect upon men and officers as they lay on their faces hugging the ground. The torments of this trying situation were almost unbearable, but it was obvious to all that it was necessary to have at hand a compact body of troops to repel any assault the enemy might make pending the reconstruction of the extreme right of our line, and a silent determination to stay seemed to take hold of each individual soldier; nor was this grim silence interrupted throughout the cannonade, except in one instance, when one of the regiments broke out in a lusty cheer as a startled rabbit in search of a new hiding-place safely ran the whole length of the line on the backs of the men.

While my troops were still lying here, General Rosecrans, with a part of his staff and a few orderlies, rode out on the rearranged line to supervise its formation and encourage the men, and in prosecution of these objects moved around the front of my column of attack, within range of the batteries that were shelling us so viciously. As he passed to the open ground on my left, I joined him. The enemy seeing this mounted party, turned his guns upon it, and his accurate aim was soon rewarded, for a solid shot carried away the head of Colonel Garesche, the chief-of-staff, and killed or wounded two or three orderlies. Garesche's appalling death stunned us all, and a momentary expression of horror spread over Rosecrans's face; but at such a time the importance of self-control was vital, and he pursued his course with an appearance of indifference, which, however, those immediately about him saw was assumed, for undoubtedly he felt most deeply the death of his friend and trusted staff-officer.

No other attacks were made on us to the east of the railroad for the rest of the afternoon, and just before dark I was directed to withdraw and take up a position along the west side of the Nashville pike,

...

...when daylight came again the skirmishers and lines of battle were in about the same position they had taken up the evening before. Soon after daybreak it became evident that the conflict was to be renewed, and a little later the enemy resumed the offensive by an attack along my left front, especially on Walker's brigade. His attempt was ineffectual, however, and so easily repulsed as to demonstrate that the desperate character of his assaults the day before had nearly exhausted his strength. About 3 o'clock in the afternoon he made another feeble charge on my front, but our fire from the barricades and rifle-pits soon demoralized his advancing lines, which fell back in some confusion, thus enabling us to pick up about a hundred prisoners. From this time till the evening of January 3 Bragg's left remained in our front, and continued to show itself at intervals by weak demonstrations, which we afterward ascertained were directly intended to cover the desperate assault he made with Breckenridge on the left of Rosecrans, an assault that really had in view only a defensive purpose, for unless Bragg dislodged the troops which were now massing in front of his right he would be obliged to withdraw General Polk's corps behind Stone River and finally abandon Murfreesboro'. The sequel proved this to be the case; and the ill-judged assault led by Breckenridge ending in entire defeat, Bragg retired from Murfreesboro' the night of January 3.

...

My effective force in the battle of Stone River was 4,154 officers and men. Of this number I lost 1,633 killed, wounded, and missing, or nearly 40 per cent. In the remaining years of the war, though often engaged in most severe contests, I never experienced in any of my commands so high a rate of casualties. The ratio of loss in the whole of Rosecrans's army was also high, and Bragg's losses were almost equally great. Rosecrans carried into the action about 42,000 officers and men. He lost 13,230, or 31 per cent. Bragg's effective force was 37,800 officers and men; he lost 10,306, or nearly 28 percent.

After the battle, Sheridan had the unhappy task of punishing officers who had behaved with cowardice during the fight.

During the engagement there had been little straggling, and my list of missing was small and legitimate; still, it was known that a very few had shirked their duty, and an example was necessary. Among this small number were four officers who, it was charged, had abandoned their colors and regiments. When their guilt was clearly established, and as soon as an opportunity occurred, I caused the whole division to be formed in a hollow square, closed in mass, and had the four officers marched to the centre, where, telling them that I would not humiliate any officer or soldier by requiring him to touch their disgraced swords, I compelled them to deliver theirs up to my colored servant, who also cut from their coats every insignia of rank. Then, after there had been read to the command an order from army headquarters dismissing the four from the service, the scene was brought to a close by drumming the cowards out of camp. It was a mortifying spectacle, but from that day no officer in that division ever abandoned his colors.

In Search of a Comfortable Way to Travel

During the summer of 1863, Sheridan took part in the Tullahoma Campaign. This was a ten day campaign during which the Union forces under General Rosecrans were able to push the Confederate forces under General Bragg out of Middle Tennessee.

It was a long campaign, and as it ended General Sheridan decided he didn't want to ride his horse back to camp. He had what he thought was a much better idea of how to get there.

Nothing further could now be done, so I instructed Watkins to rejoin the division at Cowan, and being greatly fatigued by the hard campaigning of the previous ten days, I concluded to go back to my camp in a more comfortable way than on the back of my tired horse. In his retreat the enemy had not disturbed the railway track at all, and as we had captured a hand-car at Cowan, I thought I would have it brought up to the station near the University to carry me down the mountain to my camp, and, desiring company, I persuasively invited Colonel Frank T. Sherman to ride with me. I sent for the car by a courier, and for a long time patiently awaited its arrival, in fact, until all the returning troops had passed us, but still it did not come. Thinking it somewhat risky to remain at the station without protection, Sherman and myself started our horses to Cowan by our orderlies, and set out on foot to meet the car, trudging along down the track in momentary expectation of falling in with our private conveyance. We had not gone very far before night overtook us, and we then began to realize the dangers surrounding us, for there we were alone and helpless, tramping on in the darkness over an unknown railroad track in the enemy's country, liable on the one hand to go tumbling through some bridge or trestle, and on the other, to possible capture or death at the hands of the guerrillas then infesting these mountains. Just after dark we came to a little cabin near the track, where we made bold to ask for water, notwithstanding the fact that to disclose ourselves to the inmates might lead to fatal consequences. The water was kindly given, but the owner and his family were very much exercised lest some misfortune might befall us near their house, and be charged to them, so they encouraged us to move on with a frankness inspired by fear of future trouble to themselves.

At every turn we eagerly hoped to meet the hand-car, but it never came, and we jolted on from tie to tie for eleven weary miles, reaching Cowan after midnight, exhausted and sore in every muscle from frequent falls on the rough, unballasted road-bed. Inquiry developed that the car had been well manned, and started to us as ordered, and nobody could account for its non-arrival. Further investigation next day showed, however, that when it reached the foot of the mountain, where the railroad formed a junction, the improvised crew, in the belief no doubt that the University was on the main line instead of near the branch to Tracy City, followed the main stem until it carried them clear across the range down the Crow Creek Valley, where the party was captured.

I had reason to remember for many a day this foolish adventure, for my sore bones and bruised muscles, caused me physical suffering until I left the Army of the Cumberland the next spring; but I had still more reason to feel for my captured men, and on this account I have never ceased to regret that I so thoughtlessly undertook to rejoin my troops by rail, instead of sticking to my faithful horse.

CHAPTER SEVEN

ADVENTURES TO THE ADVENTUROUS

— JOHN SINGLETON MOSBY —

*F*rom January 1863, until the end of the war, Union troops in the Shenandoah Valley of northern Virginia lived in fear of the "Gray Ghost."

Colonel John Singleton Mosby was one of the most daring commanders of the Civil War. He operated behind enemy lines with a small force capturing men, weapons, animals, supplies, and anything else he could carry off from the Union Army (on one raid, they even captured a Union General). After a raid, Mosby and his men would seemingly disappear, melting into the surrounding community of sympathetic Virginians.

His activity even struck fear into the Union high command. When General "Fighting Joe" Hooker testified before Congress, he mentioned Mosby and said that, "From the time I took command of the Army of the Potomac there was no evidence that any force of the enemy, other than that above named [Mosby's Rangers], was within 100 miles of Washington City; and yet, the planks on the chain bridge were taken up at night during the greater part of the winter and spring." Apparently they were afraid that Mosby might decide to make a raid on Washington D.C. itself.

The area in which he and his men operated is still known, even 150 years after the war, as Mosby's Confederacy. Following are just a few good stories[11] of the exploits of Mosby and his men.

The Ride around McClellan

Colonel John S. Mosby.

One of the great cavalry actions of the Civil War was the "ride around McClellan" by Confederate cavalry under the command of General J. E. B. Stuart. This was done as McClellan and his army bore down on Richmond during the Peninsular Campaign of 1862. The plan to make the raid around the Union Army was the brainchild of young Lieutenant Mosby.

In June (1862) McClellan was astraddle of the Chickahominy; his right rested on the Pamunkey, but there was a gap of several miles between his left and the James. The two armies were so close to each other that the cavalry was of little use, and it was therefore kept in the rear.

One morning I was at breakfast with Stuart, and he said that he wanted to find out if McClellan was fortifying on the Totopotomy, a creek that empties into the Pamunkey. I was glad to go for him and started off with three men. But we

---

[11] Taken from *The Memoirs of Colonel John S. Mosby*, edited by Charles Wells Russell, 1917.

found a flag of truce on the road and turned off to scout in another direction — I did not want to go back without doing something. We did not get the information for which we were sent, but we did get intelligence of even more value. We penetrated McClellan's lines and discovered that for several miles his right flank had only cavalry pickets to guard his line of communication with his depot at the White House on the Pamunkey. Here, it seemed to me, was an opportunity to strike a blow. McClellan had not anticipated any such move and had made no provision against it.

On discovering the conditions, I hastened back to Stuart and found him sitting in the front yard. It was a hot day — I was tired and lay down on the grass to tell him what I had learned. A martinet would have ordered me to stand in his presence. He listened to my story and, when I had finished, told me to go to the adjutant's office and write it down. At the same time he ordered a courier to get ready to go with him to General Lee's headquarters. I did as he requested and brought him a sheet of paper with what I had written. After reading it, Stuart called my attention to its not being signed. I signed it, although I had thought he only wanted a memorandum of what I had said — General Lee had never heard of me. Stuart took the paper and went off with a courier at a gallop. As soon as he returned, orders were issued to the cavalry to be ready.

General Lee's instructions authorizing the expedition were dated June 11. I had reported the day before. On the morning of the twelfth, with 1200 cavalry and two pieces of artillery, Stuart passed through Richmond and took the road towards Ashland. I was at headquarters when Stuart was leaving. The officer in charge asked him when he would be back. His an-

swer was, "It may be for years, it may be forever." His spirits
were buoyant.

The column moved on to Old Church in Hanover where
two squadrons of U. S. regular cavalry were stationed under
the command of Captain Royall. When the pickets were
chased in, Royall heard the firing and went to their support.
He had no cause to suspect the numbers he was meeting, for
McClellan had never even considered the possibility of a force
breaking through his lines and passing around him. A squadron of the Ninth Virginia Cavalry led our column. Captain
Latané was in command. A charge was ordered, and in the
combat Royall was wounded and routed, and Latané was
killed. We could not stay to give him even a hasty burial. Our
forces soon had possession of the abandoned camp and, as the
enemy had had no time to pack up, there was a festival.

We were now on the flank of the enemy but nine miles
from the railroad which was his line of communication. The
question which Stuart had to determine was whether to go on
or turn back. We were near the Pamunkey, and if we kept on,
the road would soon be closed behind us. The only way of
return would then be to pass around McClellan. I felt great
anxiety for fear that Stuart would halt, for I realized that there
was a chance for him to do something that had never been
done. His decision to go on showed that he possessed true military genius.

Just before Stuart gave the order for us to move, he turned
to me and said, "I want you to go on some distance ahead."
"Very well," said I, "but give me a guide." Two soldiers who
knew the roads were ordered to go with me. I was proud to be
selected for such a duty and was full of enthusiasm. We had
not gone far before Stuart sent one of his staff to tell me to go

faster and increase the distance between us. As we jogged along two miles in advance of the column, we came upon a sutler's wagon. It was filled with so many tempting things which we had not seen for nearly two years that we felt as if the blockade had been raised. We exercised the belligerent right of search. At the same time I could see, about a mile away in the Pamunkey River, a forest of masts of schooners which were unloading supplies into a train of wagons ready to carry them to the army. So I sent one man back to tell Stuart to hurry and capture the prizes and put the other as a guard over the sutler. I then went on alone. When Stuart came up, he sent a squadron to burn the schooners and the wagon train. Capturing watercraft was a novel experiment in cavalry tactics. At a bend in the road, I came upon a vidette and a sutler's wagon; they submitted quietly. Just then a bugle sounded, and I saw a body of cavalry a few hundred yards away. Fugitives from the camp we had captured had given the alarm, and the second troop was getting ready to leave. As soon as the head of our column appeared, the enemy's force at once disappeared.

About sundown we reached the York River Railroad, and the column still went on. The only way to get back to Richmond was now to recross the Chickahominy near its mouth and pass by McClellan's left flank. As some evidence of the consternation that prevailed among the Union troops, I remember that, after we left the camp, a sergeant and twenty-five men of the regular cavalry followed on under a flag of truce and surrendered to the rearguard. That night was a feast for Stuart's cavalry. On all the roads were burning trains with supplies and sutlers' goods. Champagne and Rhine wine flowed copiously.

A force was sent in pursuit of us under the command of General St. George Cooke — Stuart's father-in-law. Although the march of our column was slow, we never saw an armed foe after we left Royall's camp, except a small guard at the railroad. General Warren, who commanded a brigade behind us, said, "It was impossible for the infantry to overtake him and as the cavalry did not move without us, it was impossible for them to overtake him." Fitz-John Porter regretted that "When General Cooke did pursue, he should have tied his legs with the infantry command." As there were six cavalry regiments, including all the regulars, with a battery, on our track, it is hard to see why they wanted infantry.

Although more than forty-eight hours elapsed between the time when we passed McClellan's right flank and back around his left, he made no attempt to intercept us. In making the circuit of his army, the Confederate column was at all times within five or six miles of his headquarters, with two navigable rivers enclosing it, and another river over which we had to build a bridge in order to cross. McClellan was a soldier of great organizing ability and trained in the science of war — I mean in those operations that can be regulated by rules. But he had none of the inspiration that decides and acts instantly, and he was now confronted by a condition without a precedent. So he was helpless.

About daylight we reached a ford of the Chickahominy, a narrow crooked stream which meanders between the Pamunkey and the James. We had crossed it on the morning before. Stuart had expected to be able to ford this stream, but at this point it was overflowing. A guide told us of a bridge a mile below — or where one had been — so the column was headed for that point. When we got there, we found that the bridge was gone, although the piles were standing. Nearby were the remains of an old warehouse, which furnished material for building another. It was soon constructed — it seemed to rise out of the water by magic. It may not have been so good a bridge as Caesar threw over the Rhine, but it answered our purpose. ... When we reached Westover, the command was halted to rest and get forage, for we knew that the road to Richmond was open. Stuart now left Fitz Lee in command and rode on to report to General Lee. The column moved on by moonlight and at daybreak was in sight of Richmond. The game was won.

I had ridden several miles ahead of the column and met Stuart returning. Of course, he was delighted to hear that the cavalry was safe.

To excuse himself for what he had not done, McClellan, in a dispatch, tried to belittle this affair by saying that Stuart's cavalry did nothing but gain a little *éclat*; but it can be said with more truth that he himself lost a good deal. It was the first blow at his reputation.

The Comte de Paris, one of McClellan's staff officers, said with more truth, "They had, in point of fact, created a great commotion, shaken the confidence of the North in McClellan, and made the first experiment in those great cavalry expeditions which subsequently played so novel and important a part during the war."

Birth of a Partisan

In the winter of 1862-'63, Mosby was launched on his new course as a partisan commander, and a legend was born. Early on, not every raid went as smoothly as could be wished; then again, some went extremely well...

To relieve the monotony Stuart resolved to take his cavalry on a Christmas raid to Dumfries on Burnside's line of communication with Washington. A good many wagons with supplies were captured, and we chased a cavalry regiment through their own camp and got all their good things. There is a dispatch in the history of the telegraph in the war from an operator in Fairfax, which says, "The 17th Pennsylvania Cavalry just passed here, furiously charging to the rear."

When he returned, Stuart let me stay behind a few days with six men to operate on the enemy's outposts. He was so satisfied with our success that he let me have fifteen men to return and begin my partisan life in northern Virginia — which closed with the war. That was the origin of my battalion. On January 24, 1863, we crossed the Rappahannock and immediately began operations in a country which Joe Johnston had abandoned a year before. It looked as though I was leading a forlorn hope, but I was never discouraged. In general my purpose was to threaten and harass the enemy on the border and in this way compel him to withdraw troops from his front to guard the line of the Potomac and Washington. This would greatly diminish his offensive power.

...

Recruits came to us from inside the enemy's lines, and they brought valuable information. Then, I had picketed for some time in Fairfax the year before and had acquired considerable local knowledge. The troops attached to the defence of Washington, south of the Potomac, were distributed in winter quarters through Fairfax County and extended in an arc of a circle from the upper to the lower Potomac. The headquarters of General Stoughton, who commanded them, were at the Court House. In a day or so after I arrived in Loudoun, we began operations on the outposts of Fairfax. The weak points were generally selected for attack. Up to that time the pickets had passed a quiet life in their camps or dozing on the picket posts, but now they were kept under arms and awake all night by a foe who generally assailed them where he was least expected. At first they accounted for our attacks on the theory that the farmers and cripples they saw in the daytime ploughing their fields and taking care of their flocks collected in bands at night, raided their camps, and dispersed at daybreak. But when they went around at night searching the homes for these invisible foes, they generally found the old farmers in bed, and when they returned to camp, they often found that we had paid them a visit in their absence. The farmers could prove an alibi.

An English officer, Colonel Percy Wyndham, a soldier of fortune who had been with Garibaldi in Italy, commanded the cavalry brigade and had charge of the outposts. He was familiar with the old rules of the schools, but he soon learned that they were out of date, and his experience in war had not taught him how to counteract the forays and surprises that kept his men in the saddle all the time. The loss of sleep is irritating to anybody and, in his vexation at being struck by and striking at an invisible foe, he sent me a message calling me a horse thief. I did not deny it, but retorted that all the horses I had stolen had riders, and that the riders had sabres, carbines, and pistols. There was a new regiment in his brigade that was armed only with sabres and obsolete carbines. When we attacked them with revolvers, they were really defenceless. So I sent him word through a citizen that the men of that regiment were not worth capturing, and he must give them six- shooters. We used neither carbines nor sabres, but all the men carried a pair of Colt pistols. We did not pay for them but the U. S. Government did.

...

During the first days as a partisan, there were more comic than tragic elements in the drama of war. About that time occurred an episode that would have furnished Goldsmith with all the elements of a comedy. It was a dark night with a deep snow on the ground, but the weather was warm and the snow soft. I received information that there was a pretty strong outpost on a certain road in Fairfax, and I was determined to capture it. Of course, the fine horses were a great attraction. Several citizens had joined my command and acted as guides. Near the post lived a man named Ben Hatton, who traded in the camps and was pretty familiar with them. So, around midnight, we stopped at his house about a mile from the picket post, and he told us that he had been there that evening — I suppose to get coffee and sugar. Ben was impressed as a guide to conduct us to the rear of the enemy. When we reached that point, I determined to dismount, leave our horses, and attack on foot. Ben had fully discharged his duty and, as he was a non-combatant, I did not want to expose him to unnecessary danger. The blazing fire by which the Yankees were sleeping and dreaming was sufficient for us. So the horses were tied to the trees, and two of my men — Jimmie, an Irishman, and another we called "Coonskin", from the cap he wore — stayed with Ben as a guard over the horses.

Walking on the soft snow, we made no noise and were soon upon the picket post. The surprise was complete, and they had no time to prepare for resistance. We were soon ready to start back with our prisoners and their horses, when a fire opened in our rear, where we had left the guard and horses. The best scheme seemed to be to mount the Yankee horses, dash back, and recapture our own. Some of the men were left to bring the prisoners on foot. A considerable fusillade had been going on where the guard had been left, but it ceased suddenly when we got near the place. To our surprise we found the horses all standing hitched to the trees, and Ben Hatton lying in a snowbank, shot through the thigh. But neither "Coonskin" nor Jimmie was there. Ben told us that the Yankees had come up and attacked them; that was all he knew, except that they had shot him. He did not know whether the Yankees had carried off Jimmie and "Coonskin", or whether they had carried off the Yankees, nor could he explain why the horses were there. That was a mystery nobody could solve. We mounted; Ben was lifted on a horse behind one of the men, and we started off with all the horses and prisoners. By that time the Yankees from the camp had been attracted by the firing. They came up and opened fire at us at long range, but let us leave without venturing to come near. Ben was bleeding profusely, but it was only a flesh wound. We left him at home, curled up in bed, with his wife to nurse him. He was too near the enemy's lines for me to give him surgical assistance, and he was afraid to ask any from the camps. The wound would have betrayed him to the Yankees had they known about it, and Ben would have been hung as a spy! He was certainly innocent, for he had no desire to serve anyone but himself. His wound healed, but the only reward he got was the glory of shedding his blood for his country.

As soon as it was daylight, a strong body of cavalry was sent up the turnpike to catch us — they might as well have been chasing a herd of antelope. We had several hours' start of them, and they returned to camp in the evening, leading a lot of broken-down horses. The pursuit had done them more harm than our attack.

We brought off "Coonskin's" and Jimmie's horses, but we couldn't invent a theory to solve the mystery. Two days afterwards, "Coonskin" and Jimmie reappeared. They had trudged twenty-five miles through the snow, arriving within a few hours of each other, but from opposite directions, and each thought he was the only survivor. Neither knew that Ben Hatton had been shot, and each said that he had fought until they saw a body of Yankees riding down upon them. Then they ran off and left the horses in the belief that we were all prisoners.

By a comparison of their statements, I found out that the facts were about as follows. To keep themselves warm, the three had walked around among the trees and got separated. "Coonskin" saw Ben and Jimmie moving in the shadows and took them for Yankees. He opened on them and drew blood at the first fire. Ben yelled and fell. Jimmie took it for granted that "Coonskin" was a Yankee and returned his fire. So they were firing at each other and dodging among the trees when they saw us coming up at a gallop. As we had left them on foot, they could not understand how we could come back on horseback. So after wounding Ben Hatton and shooting at each other, they had run away from us.

...

When we captured prisoners, it was my custom to examine them apart, and in this way, together with information gained from citizens, I obtained a pretty accurate knowledge of conditions in the enemy's camps. After a few weeks of partisan life, I meditated a more daring enterprise than any I had attempted and fortunately received aid from an unexpected quarter. A deserter from the Fifth New York Cavalry, named

Ames, came to me. He was a sergeant in his regiment and came in his full uniform. I never cared to inquire what his grievance was. The account he gave me of the distribution of troops and the gaps in the picket lines coincided with what I knew and tended to prepossess me in his favor. But my men were suspicious of his good faith and rather thought that he had been sent to decoy me with a plausible story. At first I did not give him my full confidence but accepted him on probation. Ames stood all tests, and until he was killed I never had a more faithful follower.

Ames had come out from his camp on foot and proposed to me that he would go back into his camp and return on horseback, if I would accept him. A recruit, Walter Frankland, had just come to me, but he was not mounted. With my approval he agreed to go with Ames to get a horse. They trudged on foot through the snow — twenty-five miles — entered the camp of the Fifth New York Cavalry at night, unchallenged, and rode out on fine horses.

...

I now determined to execute my scheme to capture both General Stoughton and Wyndham at their headquarters [Fairfax Court House], Ames, about whose fidelity there was no longer any question, knew where their headquarters were, and the place was familiar to me as I had been in camp there. I also knew, both from Ames and the prisoners, where the gaps in the lines were at night. The safety of the enterprise lay in its novelty; nothing of the kind had been done before.

On the evening of March 8, 1863, in obedience to orders, twenty-nine men met me at Dover, in Loudoun County. None knew my objective point, but I told Ames after we started. I remember that I got dinner that day with Colonel Chancellor, who lived near Dover. Just as I was about to mount my horse, as I was leaving, I said to him, "I shall mount the stars to-night or sink lower than plummet ever sounded." I did not rise as high as the stars, but I did not sink. I then had no reputation to lose, even if I failed, and I remembered the motto, "Adventures to the adventurous."

...

It was pitch dark when we got near the cavalry pickets at Chantilly — five or six miles from the Court House. At Centreville, three miles away on the Warrenton pike and seven miles from the Court House, were several thousand troops. Our problem was to pass between them and Wyndham's cavalry without giving the alarm. Ames knew where there was a break in the picket lines between Chantilly and Centreville, and he led us through this without a vidette seeing us. After passing the outpost the chief point in the game was won. I think no man with me, except Ames, realized that we were inside the enemy's lines. But the enemy felt secure and was as ignorant as my men. The plan had been to reach the Court House by midnight so as to get out of the lines before daybreak, but the column got broken in the dark and the two parts travelled around in a circle for an hour looking for each other. After we closed up, we started off and struck the pike between Centreville and the Court House. But we turned off into the woods when we got within two or three miles of the village, as Wyndham's cavalry camps were on the pike. We entered the village from the direction of the railroad station. There were a few sentinels about the town, but it was so dark that they could not distinguish us from their own people. Squads were detailed to go around to the officers' quarters and to the stables for the horses. The courthouse yard was the rendezvous where all were to report. As our great desire was to capture Wyndham, Ames was sent with a party to the house in which he knew Wyndham had his quarters. But fortune was in Wyndham's favor that time, for that evening he had gone to Washington by train. But Ames got his two staff officers, his horses, and his uniform. One of the officers, Captain Barker, had been Ames's captain. Ames brought him to me and seemed to take great pride in introducing him to me as his former captain.

When the squads were starting around to gather prisoners and horses, Joe Nelson brought me a soldier who said he was a guard at General Stoughton's headquarters. Joe had also pulled the telegraph operator out of his tent; the wires had been cut. With five or six men I rode to the house, now the Episcopal rectory, where the commanding general was. We dismounted and knocked loudly at the door. Soon a window above was opened, and someone asked who was there. I answered, "Fifth New York Cavalry with a dispatch for General Stoughton." The door was opened and a staff officer. Lieutenant Prentiss, was before me. I took hold of his nightshirt, whispered my name in his ear, and told him to take me to General Stoughton's room. Resistance was useless, and he obeyed. A light was quickly struck, and on the bed we saw the general sleeping as soundly as the Turk when Marco Bozzaris waked him up. There was no time for ceremony, so I drew up the bedclothes, pulled up the general's shirt, and gave him a spank on his bare back, and told him to get up. As his staff officer was standing by me, Stoughton did not realize the situation and thought that somebody was taking a rude familiarity with him. He asked in an indignant tone what all this meant. I told him that he was a prisoner, and that he must get up quickly and dress.

I then asked him if he had ever heard of "Mosby", and he said he had.

"I am Mosby," I said. "Stuart's cavalry has possession of the Court House; be quick and dress."

He then asked whether Fitz Lee was there. I said he was, and he asked me to take him to Fitz Lee — they had been together at West Point. Two days afterwards I did deliver him to Fitz Lee at Culpeper Court House. My motive in trying to deceive Stoughton was to deprive him of all hope of escape and to induce him to dress quickly. We were in a critical situation, surrounded by the camps of several thousand troops with several hundred in the town. If there had been any concert between them, they could easily have driven us out; but not a shot was fired although we stayed there over an hour. As soon as it was known that we were there, each man hid and took care of himself. Stoughton had the reputation of being a brave soldier, but a fop. He dressed before a looking-glass as carefully as Sardanapalus did when he went into battle. He forgot his watch and left it on the bureau, but one of my men, Frank Williams, took it and gave it to him. Two men had been left to guard our horses when we went into the house. There were several tents for couriers in the yard, and Stoughton's horses and couriers were ready to go with us, when we came out with the general and his staff.

When we reached the rendezvous at the courtyard, I found all the squads waiting for us with their prisoners and horses. There were three times as many prisoners as my men, and each was mounted and leading a horse. To deceive the enemy and baffle pursuit, the cavalcade started off in one direction and, soon after it got out of town, turned in another. We flanked the cavalry camps, and were soon on the pike between them and Centreville. As there were several thousand troops in that town, it was not thought possible that we would go that way to get out of the lines, so the cavalry, when it started in pursuit, went in an opposite direction. Lieutenant Prentiss and a good many prisoners who started with us escaped in the dark, and we lost a great many of the horses.

A ludicrous incident occurred when we were leaving Fairfax. A window was raised, and a voice inquired, in an authoritative tone, what that cavalry was doing in the street. He was answered by a loud laugh from my men, which was notice to him that we were not his friends. I ordered several men to dismount and capture him. They burst through the front door, but the man's wife met them in the hall and held her ground like a lioness to give her husband time to escape. He was Colonel Johnstone, who was in command of the cavalry brigade during Wyndham's absence. He got out through the back door in his night clothes and barefooted, and hid in the garden. He spent some time there, as he did not know when we left, and his wife could not find him.

Our safety depended on our getting out of the Union lines before daybreak. We struck the pike about four miles from Centreville; the danger I then apprehended was pursuit by the cavalry, which was in camp behind us. When we got near the pike, I halted the column to close up. Some of my men were riding in the rear, and some on the flanks to prevent the prisoners from escaping. I left a sergeant, Hunter, in command and rode forward to reconnoitre. As no enemy was in front, I called to Hunter to come on and directed him to go forward at a trot and to hold Stoughton's bridle reins under all circumstances. Stoughton no doubt appreciated my interest in him.

With Joe Nelson I remained some distance behind. We stopped frequently to listen for the hoofbeats of cavalry in pursuit, but no sounds could be heard save the hooting of owls. My heart beat higher with hope every minute; it was the crisis of my fortunes.

...

We were now half a mile from Centreville, and the dawn was just breaking. ... [We] then turned off to go around the forts at Centreville. I rode some distance ahead of the column. The camps were quiet; there was no sign of alarm; the telegraph wires had been cut, and no news had come about our exploit at the Court House. We could see the cannon bristling through the redoubts and hear the sentinel on the parapet call to us to halt. But no attention was paid to him, and he did not fire to give the alarm. No doubt he thought that we were a body of their own cavalry going out on a scout. But soon there was a shot behind me and, turning around, I saw Captain Barker [one of the prisoners] dashing towards a redoubt and Jake, the Hungarian, close behind him and about to give him another shot, when Barker's horse tumbled and fell on him in a ditch. We soon got them out and moved on. All this happened in sight of the sentinels and in gunshot of their camps.

After we had passed the forts and reached Cub Run, a new danger was before us. The stream was swift and booming from the melting snow, and our choice was to swim, or to turn back. In full view behind us were the white tents of the enemy and the forts, and we were within cannon range. Without halting a moment, I plunged into the stream, and my horse swam to the other bank. Stoughton followed and was next to me. As he came up the bank, shivering from his cold morning bath, he said, "Captain, this is the first rough treatment I have to complain of."

Fortunately not a man or a horse was lost. When all were over, I knew there was no danger behind us, and that we were as safe as Tam O'Shanter thought he would be if he crossed the bridge of Doon ahead of the witches. I now left Hunter in charge of the column, and with one of my men, George Slater, galloped on to see what was ahead of us. I thought a force might have been sent to intercept us on the pike we had left that runs through Centreville. I did not know that Colonel Johnstone, with his cavalry, had gone in the opposite direction.

We crossed Bull Run at Sudley Ford and were soon on the historic battlefield. From the heights of Groveton we could see that the road was clear to Centreville, and that there was no pursuit. Hunter soon appeared in sight. The sun had just risen, and in the rapture of the moment I said to Slater, "George, that is the sun of Austerlitz!" I knew that I had drawn a prize in the lottery of life, and my emotion was natural and should be pardoned.

I could not but feel deep pity for Stoughton when he looked back at Centreville and saw that there was no chance of his rescue. Without any fault of his own, Stoughton's career as a soldier was blasted.

There is an anecdote told of Mr. Lincoln that, when it was reported to him that Stoughton had been captured, he remarked, with characteristic humor, that he did not mind so much the loss of a general — for he could make another in five minutes — but he hated to lose the horses.

...

War is not always grim-visaged, and incidents occur which provoke laughter in the midst of danger.

…

One night I was with one man near the enemy's camps in Fairfax. We were passing a house, when I heard a dog bark and somebody call, "Come here, Mosby." So I turned, rode up to the house, and asked the man if he had called me.

"No," he said, "I was calling Mosby. I wanted him to stop barking."

The "Greenback" Raid

Mosby's raids went on through 1863 and '64. In October of 1864, he decided to make a raid against a Union railroad. His men hit the jackpot when they found a pair of Union Paymasters aboard.

As we operated in Sheridan's rear, the railroad that brought his supplies was his weak point and consequently our favorite object of attack. For security it had to be closely guarded by detachments of troops, which materially reduced his offensive strength. We kept watch for unguarded points, and the opportunity they offered was never lost.

Early in October one of my best men, Jim Wiltshire, afterwards a prominent physician in Baltimore, discovered and reported to me a gap through which we might penetrate between the guards and reach that railroad without exciting an alarm. It was a hazardous enterprise, as there were camps along the line and frequent communication between them, but I knew it would injure Sheridan to destroy a train and compel him to place stronger guards on the road. So I resolved to take the risk. Jim Wiltshire had a time-table and we knew the minute when the train was due and so timed our arrival that we would not have to wait long.

There was great danger of our being discovered by the patrols on the road and our presence reported to the camps that were near. The situation was critical, but we were so buoyant with hope that we did not realize it. The western-bound passenger train was selected from the schedule as I knew it would create a greater sensation to burn it than any other; it was due about two o'clock in the morning. Wiltshire conducted us to a long, deep cut on the railroad. No patrol or picket was in sight. I preferred derailing the train in a cut to running it off an embankment, because there would be less danger of the passengers being hurt. People who travel on a railroad in a country where military operations are going on take the risk of all these accidents of war. I was not conducting an insurance business on life or property.

It was a lovely night, bright and clear, with a big Jack Frost on the ground. I believe that I was the only member of my command who went through the war without a watch, but all of my men had watches, and we knew it would not be long before the train would be due. Videttes were sent out, and the men were ordered to lie down on the bank of the railroad and keep quiet. We had ridden all day and were tired and sleepy, so we were soon peacefully dreaming. I laid my head in the lap of one of my men, Curg Hutchinson, and fell asleep. For some reason — I suppose it was because we were sleeping so soundly — we did not hear the train coming until it got up in the cut, and I was aroused and astounded by an explosion and a crash. As we had displaced a rail, the engine had run off the track, the boiler burst, and the air was filled with red-hot cinders and escaping steam. A good description of the scene can be found in Dante's "Inferno." Above all could be heard the screams of the passengers — especially women. The catastrophe came so suddenly that my men at first seemed to be stunned and bewildered. Knowing that the railroad guards would soon hear of it and that no time was to be lost, I ran along the line and pushed my men down the bank, ordering them to go to work pulling out the passengers and setting fire to the cars.

By this time Curg Hutchinson had recovered from the shock and had jumped on the train. When the train came up, he was snoring and dreaming that he was in Hell; and when he was awakened by the crash, he found himself breathing steam and in a sparkling shower. He had no doubt then that his dream was not all a dream. But he recovered his senses when I gave him a push, and he slid down a bank.

It did not take long to pull out the passengers. While all of this was going on, I stood on the bank giving directions to the men. One of them reported to me that a car was filled with Germans, and that they would not get out. I told him, "Set fire to the car and burn the Dutch, if they won't come out." They were immigrants going west to locate homesteads and did not understand a word of English, or what all this meant. They had through tickets and thought they had a right to keep their seats. There was a lot of New York Heralds on the train for Sheridan's army. So my men circulated the papers through the train and applied matches. Suddenly there was a grand illumination. The Germans now took in the situation and came tumbling, all in a pile, out of the flames. I hope they all lived to be naturalized and get homes. They ought not to blame me, but Sheridan; it was his business, not mine, to protect them.

While we were helping the passengers to climb the steep bank, one of my men, Cab Maddux, who had been sent off as a vidette to watch the road, came dashing up and cried out that the Yankees were coming. I immediately gave orders to mount quickly and form, and one was sent to find out if the report was true. He soon came back and said it was not. The men then dismounted and went to work again. I was very mad with Cab for almost creating a stampede and told him that I had a good mind to have him shot. Cab was quick-witted, but, seeing how angry I was, said nothing then. But he often related the circumstance after the war. His well-varnished account of it was that I ordered him to be shot at sunrise, that he said he hoped it would be a foggy morning, and that I was so much amused by his reply that I relented and pardoned him. Years afterwards Cab confessed why he gave the false alarm. He said he heard the noise the train made when it ran off the track and knew the men were gathering the spoils and did not think it was fair for him to be away picketing for their benefit. He also said that after he got to the burning cars he made up for lost time.

A great many ludicrous incidents occurred. One lady ran up to me and exclaimed, "Oh, my father is a Mason!" I had no time to say anything but, "I can't help it." One passenger claimed immunity for himself on the ground that he was a member of an aristocratic church in Baltimore.

Just as Cab dashed up, two of my men, Charlie Dear and West Aldridge, came to me and reported that they had two U. S. Paymasters with their satchels of greenbacks. Knowing it would be safer to send them out by a small party, which could easily elude the enemy, one of my lieutenants, Charlie Grogan, was detailed with two or three men to take them over the ridge to our rendezvous.

Whether my men got anything in the shape of pocketbooks, watches, or other valuable articles, I never inquired, and I was too busy attending to the destroying of the train to see whether they did. We left all the civilians, including the ladies, to keep warm by the burning cars, and the soldiers were taken with us as prisoners. Among the latter was a young German lieutenant who had just received a commission and was on his way to join his regiment in Sheridan's army. I was attracted by his personal appearance, struck up a conversation with him, and rode by him for several miles. He was dressed in a fine beaver cloth overcoat; high boots, and a new hat with gilt cord and tassel. After we were pretty well acquainted, I said to him, "We have done you no harm. Why did you come over here to fight us?" "Oh," he said, "I only come to learn de art of war." I then left him and rode to the head of the column, as the enemy were about, and there was a prospect of a fight. It was not long before the German came trotting up to join me. There had been such a metamorphosis that I scarcely recognized him. One of my men had exchanged his old clothes with him for his new ones, and he complained about it. I asked him if he had not told me that he came to Virginia to learn the art of war.

"Yes," he replied.

"Very well," I said, "this is your first lesson."

Now it must not be thought that the habit of appropriating the enemy's goods was peculiar to my men — through all ages it has been the custom of war. Not long after this incident I had to suffer from the same operation — was shot at night and stripped of my clothes. Forty years afterwards a lady returned to me the hat which I was wearing. She said that her uncle, Lieutenant-Colonel Coles of the regiment that captured it, had given it to her as a relic of the war. That is war. I am willing to admit, however, that in a statement of mutual accounts at that time my men were largely in debt to Sheridan's men.

...

The paymasters and other prisoners were sent south to prison, and one of them, Major Ruggles, died there. They were unjustly charged with being in collusion with me, but their capture was simply an ordinary incident of war. As the Government held them responsible for the loss of the funds, they had to apply to Congress for relief. After the war, Major Moore came to see me to get a certificate of the fact that I had captured the money.... The sum captured was $173,000.

...

This meant that the railroad must be more strongly guarded if communication was to be kept up between the Shenandoah Valley, Washington, and Baltimore. Troops were rushed from many points to guard the railroad and the canal. My object had then been accomplished.

A Meeting with Mosby

In April 1865, the Confederacy was crumbling, Richmond had fallen and Robert E. Lee had surrendered, but Mosby still ruled his small domain. Finally Union General Winfield Hancock made contact with Mosby and offered a meeting to negotiate the possible surrender of Mosby and his men. This is a Union Colonel's account[12] of what happened at that meeting.

At the time of the surrender of Lee and the fall of Richmond about the only confederate force in the Shenandoah Valley was Mosby's band. The last of Early's army had been

---

[12] Taken from *Personal Recollections of a Cavalryman with Custer's Michigan Cavalry Brigade in the Civil War*, by James Harvey Kidd, 1908.

swept away by Sheridan's advance, led by Custer, and for the first time since 1860, that beautiful valley was free from the movements of armed forces confronting each other in hostile array. The bold and dashing partisan was, however, capable of doing much mischief and it was thought best by General Hancock to treat with him and see if he would not consent to a cessation of hostilities and, possibly, take the parole. Accordingly, an agreement was made to meet him at Millwood, a little town a few miles distant from Winchester and near the mountains. General Chapman, a cavalry officer, was selected to conduct the negotiations and with an escort of two regiments left early on the morning of the day designated for the rendezvous agreed upon. Not yet having been relieved from duty there I readily obtained permission to accompany the expedition. I was early in the saddle and joining a party of staff officers, struck across country, arriving at about the same time as the escort which took the main road.

The region to which we were going was one of the favorite haunts of Mosby and his men and it produced a queer sensation to thus ride peacefully through a country where for four long years, the life or liberty of the union soldier caught outside the lines had been worth not a rush, unless backed by force enough to hold its own against an enemy. There never had been a time since our advent into this land of the Philistines (a land literally flowing with milk and honey) when we could go to Millwood without a fight, and here we were going without molestation, right into the lair of the most redoubtable of all the partisan leaders.

But Mosby's word was law in that section. His fiat had gone forth that there was to be a truce, and no union men were to be molested until it should be declared off. There was, therefore, no one to molest or make us afraid. No picket challenged. Not a scout or vidette was seen. The country might have been deserted, for all the indications of life that could be heard or seen. The environment seemed funereal and the ride could hardly be described as a cheerful one. Each one was busy with his own thoughts. All wondered if the end had really come, or was it yet afar off? Lee had surrendered but Johnson had not. Would he?

The chief interest, for the time being, however, centered in the coming interview with Mosby, under a flag of truce. If he could be prevailed upon to take the parole there would not be an armed confederate in that part of Virginia.

It had been expected that he would be there first but he was not and his arrival was eagerly awaited. The escort was massed near a large farm house, the owner of which was very hospitable and had arranged to give the two commands a dinner.

The officers were soon dispersed in easy attitudes about the porches and lawn or under the shade of friendly trees, smoking and chatting about the interesting situation. Eager glances were cast in the direction from which our old foe was expected to come, and there was some anxiety lest he should fail to meet the appointment after all. But, at length, when the forenoon was pretty well spent, the sound of a bugle was heard. All sprang to their feet. In a moment, the head of a column of mounted men emerged from a woody screen on the high ground, toward the east, as though coming straight out of the mountain, and presently, the whole body of gray troopers came into view.

It was a gallant sight, a thrilling scene, for all the world like a picture from one of Walter Scott's novels; and to the imagination, seemed a vision of William Wallace or of Rob Roy. The place itself was a picturesque one — a little valley nestling beneath the foot-hills at the base of the mountains whose tops towered to the sky. Hills and wooded terraces surrounded it, shutting it in on all sides, obstructing the view and leaving the details of the adjacent landscape to the imagination.

Mosby evidently had arranged his arrival with a view to theatric effect — though it was no mimic stage on which he was acting — for it was to the sound of the bugle's note that he burst into view and, like a highland chief coming to a lowland council, rode proudly at the head of his men. Finely uniformed and mounted on a thorough bred sorrel mare, whose feet spurned the ground, he pranced into our presence. Next came about sixty of his men, including most of the officers, all, like himself, dressed in their best and superbly mounted. It was a goodly sight to see.

General Chapman advanced to meet the commander as he dismounted and the two officers shook hands cordially. There were then introductions all around and in a few moments, the blue and the gray were intermingling on the most friendly terms.

It was difficult to believe that we were in the presence of the most daring and audacious partisan leader, at the same time that he was one of the most intrepid and successful cavalry officers in the confederate service. He was wary, untiring, vigilant, bold, and no federal trooper ever went on picket without the feeling that this man might be close at hand watching to take advantage of any moment of unwariness. He had been known in broad daylight, to dash right into federal camps, where he was outnumbered a hundred to one, and then make his escape through the fleetness of his horses and his knowledge of the by-roads. On more than one occasion, he had charged through a union column, disappearing on one flank as quickly as he had appeared on the other. His men, in union garb, were often in our camps mingling unsuspected with our men or riding by their side when on the march.

We were prepared to see a large, fierce-looking dragoon but, instead, beheld a small, mild-mannered man not at all like the ideal. But, though small, he was wiry, active, restless and full of fire.

"How much do you weigh, colonel?" I asked as I shook his hand and looked inquiringly at his rather slender figure.

"One hundred and twenty-eight pounds," said he.

"Well, judging from your fighting reputation, I looked for a two hundred pounder, at least," I replied.

His spare form was set off by a prominent nose, a keen eye and a sandy beard. There was nothing ferocious in his appearance' but when in the saddle he was not a man whom one would care to meet single-handed. There was that about him which gave evidence of alertness and courage of the highest order.

It was astonishing to see officers of Mosby's command walk up to union officers, salute and accost them by name.

"Where did I meet you?" would be the reply.

"There was no introduction. I met you in your camp, though you were not aware of it at the time."

Major Richards, a swarthy-looking soldier, remarked to me that he was once a prisoner of the Fifth and Sixth Michigan cavalry. He was captured near Aldie, in the spring of 1863, and made his escape when the Michigan regiments were on the march back to Fairfax Court House, in the night, when his guards were not noticing, by falling out of the column and boldly ordering his captors to "close up" as they were coming out of a narrow place in the road when the column of fours had to break by twos. In the darkness and confusion he was mistaken for one of our own officers. After he had seen the column all "closed up" he rode the other way.

After a while the farmer called us in to dinner and the blue and the gray were arranged around the table, in alternate seats. I sat between two members of the celebrated Smith family. One of them, R. Chilton Smith, was a relative of General Lee, or of his chief-of-staff, a young man of very refined manners, highly educated and well bred. He sent a package and a message by me to a friend in Winchester, a commission that was faithfully executed. The other was the son of Governor, better known as "Extra Billy" Smith, of Virginia; a short, sturdy youth, full of life and animation and venom.

"Mosby would be a blanked fool to take the parole," said he, spitefully. "I will not, if he does."

"But Lee has surrendered. The jig is up. Why try to prolong the war and cause further useless bloodshed?"

"I will never give up so long as there is a man in arms against your yankee government," he replied.

"But what can you do? Richmond is ours."

"I will go and join 'Joe' Johnston."

"It is a question of but a few days, at most, when Sherman will bag him."

"Then I will go west of the Mississippi, where Kirby Smith still holds the fort."

"Grant, Sherman, Sheridan and Thomas will make short work of Kirby Smith."

"Then, if worst comes to worst," he hotly retorted, "I will go to Mexico and join Maximilian. I will never submit to yankee rule; never."

I greatly enjoyed the young man's fervor and loyalty to his "cause" and, in spite of his bitterness, we took quite a liking to each other and, on parting, he was profuse in his expressions of regard and urged me cordially not to forget him should fortune take me his way again.

A day or two later, I was ordered to Petersburg, and soon thereafter, was in Richmond, Johnston having, in the meantime, surrendered. In the evening of the day of my arrival, after having visited the points of interest, Libby prison, the burnt district, the state house, etc., I was in the office of the Spotswood hotel where were numbers of federal and confederate soldiers chatting pleasantly together, when I was saluted with a hearty:

"Hello; how are you, colonel!" and, on looking around, was surprised as well as pleased to see my young friend of the Millwood conference.

I was mighty glad to meet him again and told him so, while he seemed to reciprocate the feeling. There was a cordial shaking of hands and after the first friendly greetings had been exchanged I said:

"But what does this mean? How about Mexico and Maximilian? Where is Mosby? What has been going on in the valley? Tell me all about it."

"Mexico be blanked" said he. "Mosby has taken the parole and so have I. The war is over and I am glad of it. I own up. I am subjugated."

The next day I met him again.

"I would be only too glad to invite you to our home and show you a little hospitality," said he, "but your military governor has taken possession of our house, father has run away, and mother is around among the neighbors."

I assured him of my appreciation of both his good will and of the situation and begged him to be at ease on my account. He very politely accompanied me in a walk around the city and did all he could to make my stay agreeable.

I never saw him afterwards. When in Yorktown in 1881, I made inquiry of General Fitzhugh Lee about young Smith and learned that he was dead. I hope that he rests in peace, for although a "rebel" and a "guerrilla," as we called them in those days, he was a whole-hearted, generous, and courageous foe who, though but a boy in years, was ready to fight for the cause he believed in and, in true chivalrous spirit, grasp the hand of his former adversary in genuine kindness and goodfellowship.

One other incident of the Millwood interview is perhaps worth narrating.

A bright eyed young scamp of Mosby's command mounted the sorrel mare ridden by his chief, and flourishing a roll of bills which they had probably confiscated on some raid into yankee territory, rode back and forth in front of the lawn, crying out:

"Here are two hundred dollars in greenbacks which say that this little, lean, sorrel mare of Colonel Mosby's, can outrun any horse in the yankee cavalry."

The bet was not taken.

Mosby decided not to surrender his command to General Hancock, and instead disbanded his men on April 21, 1865. Mosby and a few of his officers tried to join up with the Confederate Army in

North Carolina under the command of General Joseph Johnston; but Johnston surrendered his Army before Mosby reached him, and Mosby decided to return to Virginia.

Upon his return, he found that General Hancock was offering a bounty for his capture. He lived as a fugitive, avoiding capture, for several months, until General Grant intervened on Mosby's behalf and granted him a pardon.

After the war Mosby became a friend of General Grant and actively campaigned for Grant's election as President of the United States. He then served Grant's administration as the U.S Consul to Hong Kong from 1878-1885.

Later in life, Mosby moved to California where he became a friend of future World War II hero George S. Patton and his family. When Patton was a boy, the aged Mosby would help him recreate Civil War battles as they rode over the Patton Ranch together, with Patton pretending to be General Lee. Mosby passed away in May 1916, in Washington D.C.

CHAPTER EIGHT

*SAM COULD ONLY ROLL ON THE GROUND
BETWEEN HIS BURSTS OF LAUGHTER*

— THEODORE GERRISH —

*T*o me, the stories of the common soldiers are often the
most interesting. They seem to capture a side of the war
that most historians don't find important, and they took
part in many activities that it was best their officers didn't know
about...

For these kinds of tales, the writings[13] of Reverend Theodore
Gerrish are some of the best. In this chapter we will hear how he
joined the Army as a member of the famed 20th Maine, how he took
part in the hazing of both new recruits and officers, and of his experience in the heat of battle.

Joining the Army of the Potomac

*Early in the war, young Theodore joined as a Private in the
newly formed 20th Maine Volunteer Infantry Regiment. This unit
would become most famous for its defense of Little Round Top at the
Battle of Gettysburg, and for some of its officers who rose to promi-*

---

[13] Taken from *Army Life: A Privates Reminiscences of the Civil War*, by
Rev. Theodore Gerrish, 1882.

nence during the war (most notably, Adelbert Ames and Joshua Lawrence Chamberlain). When this new regiment was seen in public for the first time, however, it presented a much less glorious appearance...

On the second day of September, 1862, a regiment of uniformed, but unarmed men, marched from Camp Mason, near Portland, Maine, to the railroad depot, from whence it proceeded by rail to the city of Boston. The regiment numbered "a thousand strong"; and as we marched through the streets of Boston, the sidewalks were covered with people who were eagerly looking at us.

"Where are you from?" bawled an old salt, who stood leaning his back against a lamp-post. "From the land of spruce gum and buckwheat cakes," loudly responded a brawny backwoodsman fresh from the forests of his native state. A loud laugh rang out from the crowd. One gentleman swung his hat, and proposed "three cheers for the old pine tree state." *Hip, Hip, Hip*, and a rousing volley of cheers ran along the street for many blocks.

We soon reached the wharf, where we embarked on board the United States transport "Merrimac," a huge steamer of some three thousand tons burden.

We quickly proceeded to our new quarters "between decks," but had barely time to stow our knap sacks away in the rough berths, before we heard the sound of music and loud cheering upon the wharf, and the 36th Massachusetts regiment, a gallant body of men, twelve hundred in number, marched on board the Merrimac, and shared our quarters with us. The two regiments numbered some twenty-two hundred men, and occupied every square foot of space that the steamer afforded.

Preparations for departure were rapidly made, and soon the plank was pulled in, the lines were cast off, the great engine began to throb with a fiery life, and we glided down the harbor, — I knew not where.

With moist eyes and heart strangely throbbing, I stood in the midst of the crowd pressed against the steamer's rail, and looked toward the city, now fast receding from view, but I saw not the countless domes and spires of the great town. I did not notice the great business blocks, and heard not the rush and hum of traffic that fell upon my ear like the music of a distant waterfall. I was thinking of home, and seemed to see, like a picture on the distant sky, a great forest, a small clearing on the hillside, a little cottage home, and a circle of dear friends as they stood with tearful eyes to say good-by, as I thus took my departure from home. A sickly sensation came creeping over my heart, a great lump gathered in my throat, but just at that moment a sergeant, who sat on a huge pile of baggage, began to read a paper just purchased in the city: it contained the condensed telegrams of the preceding week — telegrams that had sent mourning and consternation all through the loyal North. "McClellan's retreat from the peninsula." "Major General John Pope assumes command of the Army." "His headquarters are to be in the saddle." "A terrible battle has been fought on the old battle-field of Bull Run, in which the union forces have been disastrously defeated." "A terrific encounter between the right of Pope's army and Stonewall Jackson at Chantilly, twenty miles from Washington, in which the Unionists are defeated." "General Stevens and brave Phil Kearney are among the slain." "Lee still advancing." "Washington is in danger." "The war to be transferred to Northern soil."

It would be difficult to describe the emotions of the listeners as the news was read. Each man comprehended the fearful situation of the army we were hastening to reinforce, but not a cheek grew pale at the thought of coming danger. A son of the old Bay State, from the hills of Berkshire, climbed up in the rigging of the steamer, and proposed three cheers for "Old Abe," and at least a thousand voices responded to the call. Three more were given for "Little Mac," and then three times three for the "red, white and blue." Men cheered until they were hoarse, the air was filled with flying caps, and the good steamer Merrimac shook from truck to keel.

Thus began my first voyage on the ocean. Everything was new and exciting to my boyish vision. The steamer's space between the decks had been filled with rude bunks, and in these we were stowed until every square foot of space was occupied, and then hundreds of men were obliged to remain on deck.

The first night was one of unnecessary alarm. Several rumors were flying. "The lower hold was said to be filled with powder and munitions of war." "And one of the Confederate privateers had been seen cruising in the vicinity within a short time. If we came in contact with her, we would be all captured, or blown to the stars, by their firing a shell into the magazine under our feet." "Some wondered what we should do if the steamer should strike a rock and go down." And thus the hours pass. The steamer rolls in the swells of the ocean. There is the sickening and monotonous roar of the machinery, and the tramp of feet overhead.

The atmosphere grows thick and foul; sleep refuses to come to my relief. At last all is still save the rumble of machinery, and the ceaseless lapping of the waves against the sides of the steamer. All are sleeping; suddenly there is a fearful crash. Fifty voices shout, "She has struck a rock." Fifteen hundred men spring from their bunks, and with a mighty surge rush for the gangway. The panic is terrible. Men push, swear, crowd, strike, and rush on, but to our horror the hatch is fastened down, and there is no escape. Then someone for the first time discovers the cause of the alarm. The boat has not struck a rock, but a long tier of bunks insecurely fastened had fallen upon the tiers below, and all had gone down together.

A general laugh followed this discovery, all declaring they had not been frightened in the least, and we returned to our bunks wiser, and I trust, braver men.

Thus days and nights passed; the weather was beautiful, and the ocean like a sea of glass.

Through the days, we studied the ever-changing sea, dotted here and there with snowy sails. We watched the flight of birds, and the playing of the fish. At night we would dream of home and friends, or of the scenes of carnage toward which we were hastening.

On the morning of September 7th our steamer drew up to a wharf at the city of Alexandria, Virginia, seven miles below Washington. At this point the Potomac River is a mile in width, and in the harbor of Alexandria the largest vessels can find anchorage.

The landing was made; our regiment disembarked, and stood for the first time upon the "sacred soil of Virginia."

...

At night we encamped near the city. Our blankets were unrolled, and we lay down to rest. The air was balmy and scented with southern mint. We were weary with the excitement of the past week. God's stars twinkled overhead as if to assure us of his protection and care. Amidst the falling shower of mist and dew we passed our first night on southern soil. At sunrise the reveille awakens us. Breakfast is eaten, and we embark on board a small steamer for Washington.

The capital of our country in 1862 but little resembled the capital of to-day.

It was the Sabbath day when we entered the city. At home it had been a day of quiet rest, or delightful worship. How strange the surroundings seemed to us as we marched along the streets of Washington. Everyone was excited over the recent defeats suffered by the Union army, and the rapid advance of General Lee.

The demoralization of war was visible on every hand. Regiments of soldiers filled the squares, squadrons of cavalry were dashing along the streets, batteries of artillery, long lines of baggage wagons and ambulances were seen in every direction. We marched to the United States Arsenal, and here everything reminded us of war. Great piles of dismounted cannon looked grimly upon us, stacks of shot and shells surrounded them, the building itself was packed with fire-arms of every design, from the old flintlock musket of continental times to the rifle of most modern make. Our regiment was equipped and armed with Enfield rifles, and there was dealt out to each man forty rounds of ammunition. We now supposed we were model soldiers, and marched proudly away. That night we encamped near the arsenal grounds.

On the 8th we were assigned to Butterfield's famous "Light Brigade," "Morrell's Division," "Porter's Corps," and late in the afternoon of that day, by the way of the long bridge, we marched to Fort Craig, on Arlington heights, to join our brigade.

It was a most ludicrous march. We had never been drilled, and we felt that our reputation was at stake. An untrained drum corps furnished us with music; each musician kept different time, and each man in the regiment took a different step. Old soldiers sneered; the people laughed and cheered; we marched, ran, walked, galloped, and stood still, in our vain endeavors to keep step. We reached our destination, joined the brigade, stacked our arms, and encamped for the night. We were now a part of the army of the Potomac.

Foraging

Soldiers foraging for food got into some very entertaining scrapes. (Think of young Mr. Stanley in search of his Christmas dinner, or General Sheridan's men discovering that not all their comrades were exactly what they seemed.) Mr. Gerrish was no different, having some narrow escapes when he went in search of the proverbial "milk and honey."

Foraging soon becomes a science in the soldiers' life. We had just entered the army, and did not understand it as well as did those who had been longer in the service, but we applied ourselves closely to the work, and soon became quite expert. We must always remember that customs in the army vary from those in civil life, and things which in the latter would not be tolerated for a moment, would be commendable in the former. Many laughable incidents occurred, which, if written, would fill volumes. While marching through Louden valley, our regiment encamped one night at a small village called "Snickersville," and the following day we remained in camp. A small squad of us sallied forth in the afternoon, without permission, "to seek whom we might devour."

Some few miles from camp, in an out-building on a large plantation, we found a very large hive of bees which appeared to be well filled with honey. Now honey and hard tack together make a most desirable diet, and we knew that we had found a prize; but, as I have already intimated, foraging was new business to us, and we were a little timid, and consequently concluded that the better way for us to pursue, was to return to camp, and then come out after dark and secure it. We returned to camp highly elated at the prospect of securing the coveted prize. Of course our comrades were to know nothing about it. We held a small council of war, and arranged our plans. Late in the evening we passed through the guard unnoticed by the sentinels, and quickly tramped over fences and across fields until we reached the plantation, and to our joy found the hive of honey as we had left it in the afternoon. It was a huge, old-fashioned affair, some four feet in height, by two and a half square. It was so heavy that it required our united strength to carry it. We soon found that "the way of the transgressor is hard." We had just passed from the building to the open yard, when a smothered exclamation from Joe, which was half way between an oath and a yell, attracted our attention; we hurriedly dropped the hive, and Joe began to make the most lively antics around the yard. We soon learned the cause; there was a small opening in the side of the hive, through which the bees had been accustomed to pass in and out. Joe had, unfortunately, placed his hand near this opening, the occupants of the hive had been aroused by their removal, and a large cluster of them had passed up under his sleeve, and intrenched themselves upon his arm. It was the first wound that he had received in the war of the rebellion. "Confound them!" muttered Joe, "I will fix them," and taking off his overcoat, a new one that he had just drawn, he proceeded to wrap it around the hive in such a manner that the opening was covered. We then lifted our burden and tugged away. We passed out beyond the barn, and reached a narrow lane inclosed on either side by a very high fence, when to our horror we heard a party of men approaching. "Here they are," cried one, leaping upon the fence. "Surrender, surrender" cried the new comers. "The provost guard," we all exclaimed together. Now if there is a thing in the world that a new soldier is afraid of, it is the provost guard. Guns rattled, we dropped the hive, overcoat and all, and sprang over the high fence and ran; our pursuers crying out that if we did not stop they would fire. At a break-neck rate we went across the broad field; a deep, wide ditch was in our way; with a most desperate leap we cleared this obstacle, and rushed on to our camp. When we arrived there we lay down together to talk over our narrow escape. We were highly elated to think that we had eluded the grasp of the much dreaded "provost guard."

If we had made a charge upon the enemy, and covered ourselves with honor, we would not have felt better than at that time. We were so much excited that we could not sleep. In about an hour we heard a commotion in the street of the adjoining company. Some men seemed to be carrying a heavy burden, while others were convulsed with laughter, which they were endeavoring vainly to suppress.

We listened; they were talking. Their whole company seemed to be gathered around them. As we listened we became disgusted. They had got our honey. They had overheard us in the afternoon as we made our plans. A squad of them had followed to make us believe they were the provost guard, and they had succeeded. We endeavored to induce Joe to ask them about his coat, but he declared that he would freeze to death like a man before he would take such a step.

The affair soon leaked out, and for six months, if any of the boys wished to silence either of us, they only had to speak the one word "honey."

...

Milk, of course, was a luxury in the army, and many were the expeditions made from the picket line at Rappahannock station to secure the coveted article. Having learned one day from a contraband that came within our lines that there was a plantation about three miles out, where several cows were kept, two of us arranged to go out and secure some milk. The only possible danger was that we might fall in with some of the rebel cavalry, who were occasionally scouting in that vicinity; but we decided, if we went out before daylight, that even this danger would be removed, and so, the next morning, about four o'clock, two of us sallied forth. I was armed with a camp kettle that would contain twenty quarts. My companion carried his rifle. The distance was greater than we anticipated, and when we reached the plantation, day was dawning. We soon ascertained that the cows were in a yard near the house. The programme was for me to enter the yard and milk the cows, while Sam was to stand guard, and give the alarm in case of danger. The cows were wild, and some little time was consumed in skirmishing around the yard before I could begin to milk. My position was such that my back was toward the house, and very near the fence that inclosed the yard. I was meeting with great success, and several quarts of the precious fluid already repaid me for my industry. I was thinking of the rebel cavalry, when, in the dim, gray light of morning, a huge form towered upon the fence above me, and sprang with ter-

rific force to my side, and at the same moment a loud, un-
earthly yell saluted my ears. I thought Moseby, and his whole
gang of cut-throats were upon us. I sprang to my feet, upset
the pail, rushed through the herd of astonished cattle, climbed
the fence, and dashed toward the picket line. After I had run
an eighth of a mile, I thought of Sam. I looked around, expecting to see a squad of the enemy following me, but to my surprise saw Sam coming, roaring with laughter, and motioning
for me to return. I returned, and demanded the cause of my
alarm. Poor Sam could only roll on the ground and ejaculate
between his bursts of laughter, "It is so good, so good." After a
time I learned that while I was milking, a colored lady of gi-
gantic proportions had come out of the house with a milk-
pail, and proceeded to the yard. Sam, from his outlook, saw
her, but she did not know of our presence. Sam saw that she
intended to climb the fence near where I was milking, and
decided that it would be a grand chance to settle some old
scores with me, and so, when she descended from her elevated
position, he had given me the benefit of the yell. It had operated in a double capacity, for the negress had rushed to the
house in a fright while I was running away. We returned to
the yard, and secured some milk. Sam promised me most sol-
emnly that the boys in camp should never hear of it, but before the close of that day it was known to every man in the
regiment.

New Recruits

*Naturally, our young hero and his fellow volunteers were not
raw recruits for long. Once they had become old hands at Army life,
they turned their attention to "breaking in" any new recruits that
joined the regiment...*

Many recruits came to us during that time, and of course they were proper subjects for practical jokes. One fellow from the backwoods of Maine reached the regiment late in the afternoon. He soon revealed to a number of the boys that his only fear in becoming a soldier was that he would not be able to stand on "a picket post." He felt that it would require a great deal of practice to do this in a skillful manner, and since he had decided to enlist, he had not had a moment's time to practice it. Of course the boys had a great deal of sympathy for him, and kindly promised to assist him, for which he was very thankful. They informed him how difficult a thing it was for them when they first began. They accompanied him to the lower end of the street, where a post some four feet in height and six inches in diameter was set upright in the ground, the upper end being sharpened nearly to a point. With a little assistance the recruit succeeded in reaching its sharpened top, and in the evening twilight, for nearly two long hours he managed to maintain his position, and received the compliments of his comrades. He then went to his tent, proud of the fact that he had mastered so difficult a problem in so brief a time.

Another recruit, fresh from the schools and refined society, but who had never seen much of the world, came to our company. The boys saw at a glance that he was a glorious subject for a practical joke, and anxiously waited for an opportunity. It soon came. The young man was very confidential, and before he had been with us a whole day revealed all his plans. He had enlisted, knowing that his education and polished manners would give him rapid promotion. Of course he would be a private but a few weeks, so he had brought an officer's uniform with him, and had the whole suit packed in his knapsack.

Seeing that we were deeply interested in his plans, he asked if we could advise him in any way that would assist in his promotion; he would do anything to gain success in that line. Various things were spoken of by his advisers, which, if done, might aid him in his commendable ambition. One remarked that extravagance in the use of government stores was the great evil of the army, and when the officers noticed that a man was prudent, and looked out for the interests of the Government, he was always rapidly promoted. We all took the hint. Only the day before this conversation, fresh ammunition had been issued to our regiment, and that which we had carried so long having become worthless by exposure to air and moisture, was thrown away. The cartridges were scattered along the street and through our tents. "Yes, that is so," continued another, "now, there are those cartridges; it is too bad to have them wasted, and I have no doubt the colonel would promote any man who would gather them up and carry them to his tent, but I won't do it." "Neither will I," said speaker number three, "I enlisted to shoot rebels; I am perfectly willing to wade in blood, but I won't do such work as that if I am never promoted." After this patriotic declaration he yawned, and turned over in his berth as if he would sleep; but the bait had been swallowed. The recruit glided from the little group of soldiers, went to the cook house, borrowed two large camp kettles, and then through the tents and streets he went, until the kettles were nearly filled with cartridges, and he had all the load he could possibly carry. Then staggering along with a kettle in each hand, he walked to the colonel's tent. He passed the guard who was on duty there, and did not halt until he had reached the doorway. He then gave a smart knock, with the assurance of one who is confident of receiving a warm welcome. One of the field officers answered the summons. The expectant recruit made known his business. The officer glanced down the street and saw the laughing soldiers. He took in the whole situation at a glance. There was a scowl, an oath, a vanishing officer, a door closing with a fearful slam, and Company H yelled and howled with delight. The sounds of merriment must have grated harshly upon the ears of the poor fellow who had been the victim. This episode crushed his expectations, and we never heard him utter the word promotion again.

Picket Duty

The "practical jokes" were not confined to the ranks either. When the men didn't like the behavior of their officers, they might find ways to make the lives of those in command difficult as well...

As already stated, during the winter we were encamped at Rappahannock station, our picket duty was light. And as there was evidently no enemy in our immediate front, this duty was far more pleasant than that which usually falls to the soldier's lot. The usual rigor and discipline was much relaxed. A corporal and three men would be placed upon each post, and around a good fire of oak logs the hours passed pleasantly away. The practical jokes and fun were not confined to the camp, but were often indulged in on the picket line. As we look back to those months we smile as we remember how often we were made the victims of our comrades' wit. No opportunity for fun was ever allowed to pass unimproved, no matter whether the victim was an officer or a private. There was an officer in our brigade who was distinguished throughout the command as an ardent admirer of "red tape," or, to use the phrase coined by the boys for the occasion: "He was always on his military." When this officer was in command of the picket line there was no comfort or rest for himself or any other person. At such times he evidently comprehended the vast responsibilities that rested upon him, and acted accordingly. He would be up at all hours of the night, prowling along the picket line, evidently hoping to find some luckless fellow asleep. If a sentinel failed to challenge him, as laid down in the "tactics," woe be unto him. He would not allow four of us to remain upon a single post and relieve each other, as the other officers did. The regulation plan of the reliefs tramping the length of the line to relieve the men each two hours must be carried out. No sentry was allowed to have a fire on his post, and the reserve picket forces must sleep on their arms, to be ready at a moment's warning in case the enemy should advance. Thus for three days and nights he would strut and parade along the picket line, and each man would sputter, growl and swear at such a display. Each one felt inspired to vex and aggravate him as much as possible, without committing any act for which he could be punished. One night, in the month of March, 1864, I was on picket, and this officer was in charge of the line. He had established his headquarters, with the reserve, in a piece of oak woods about one-third of a mile in rear of the picket line. For two days he had been in charge, making it just as uncomfortable as he could for the men. The rain had been falling in torrents, but the storm had now cleared away. The stars shone down through the mists, and their feeble light partially dispelled the darkness and gloom. The air was damp and chilly, and a thick fog enveloped us like a mantle. The ground was soft and muddy. This officer had passed along the line after dark, and given orders for every man to be on the watch, to exercise a double caution, for he had no doubt but that Moseby's guerrillas would attack our line before morning. The reserve were ordered to "fall in," and were then commanded to sleep on their arms and be ready to repel the enemy. Every soldier knew that, in all probability, there was not a rebel within ten miles, and that this was only an exhibition of "red tape." My relief went on at eleven o'clock, to remain two hours. I had been standing in the darkness about an hour when a soldier on the adjoining post spoke my name in a low voice. I went to where he was standing and found that he was a recruit who had recently joined our regiment, and that this was his first service on picket. He told me that he had been standing there for three hours. The relief must have passed him in the darkness, and he was nearly frozen. He was very angry, and denounced the corporal for thus passing him, saying it was simply an old soldier's trick played upon him because he was a recruit; but he wanted them to all understand that, although he had just enlisted, he was not a simpleton. When he had finished his tirade, he asked me what would be the most effectual method of arousing the corporal and also of informing the commanding officer of the situation. He was evidently determined to have the corporal court-martialed, and thus teach the old soldiers a lesson. I, of course, gave him the information he needed, and informed him that if he should fire his gun he would probably arouse the corporal, and also have a chance to state the facts to the officer in charge. I then hastened back to my post. A moment after, a flash of fire glared through the gloom, there was the sharp crack of a rifle, and a minie-ball went whistling forth in the darkness. For a moment all was still, and then there was an excitement. Clear and shrill I heard the officer's voice ring out through the forest, "Fall in!" "Fall in!" There was a rattle of bayonets as the guns were hastily taken from the stacks, and then "Forward!" "Double-quick!" "March!" and one hundred men under the command of this irrepressible officer came dashing out toward the picket line. The officer was on horseback, and his steed sank deep in the mud at every plunge. In this ludicrous condition they bore down upon the picket post where I was standing. There was no time to lose. Twisting the laugh from my features, I prepared for the desperate work of halting the charging column, and with all my power yelled, "Halt! Who comes there?" The officer informed me of his rank, but of course I must receive the countersign over the point of the bayonet, at such a perilous time, before I could believe him, and to do this he must dismount in the mud. He gave the magic word, and then inquired about the firing. I told him it was down on our left, and that evidently our man had fired at some object, or else some person had fired at him. In a moment he was mounted and leading on his command. Again he was challenged, this time by the offender himself. "Who fired that gun?" roared the officer. "I did," answered the enraged soldier. "At what did you fire?" "Nothin', sir," was the reply, "only I have stood here three hours and want to be relieved." The men chuckled aloud with laughter. The officer was speechless with rage, and demanded, "How long have you been in the service?" "Four days," responded the veteran. There was no remedy. The man was a recruit and knew no better. The officer summoned the corporal and ordered him to instruct the man how he could be relieved from his duty without firing his rifle. He then rode slowly back to his tent, and we all fancied that from that hour he was more of a man than he had ever been before.

Battle

Army life wasn't all practical jokes and foraging adventures, however. There was also the bloody work of battle, and Mr. Gerrish saw his share of that as well.

This first account tells the story of a skirmish he was involved in while the Union Army was pressing the Confederate retreat after the Battle of Antietam.

On the 19th of September, two days after this battle was fought, there was great excitement in our regiment, as we were ordered to cross the Potomac, and follow up the retreat of General Lee. This was to be a new experience to us. Up to this time we had not been in the advance. We had seen our comrades fight and go down in the smoke of battle, but now we were to experience that which hitherto we had only seen.

The regiment quickly obeyed the order to "fall in." Then the command "by the right flank, march," was given, and away we went. We soon reached the Potomac River, and crossed at the Shepherdstown fords. The river was wide, the water deep, the current swift, and the ledges upon which we walked were so narrow that our crossing was necessarily very slow; but we finally reached the Virginia shore.

Not a gun had been fired, and not an enemy had been seen. Our regimental line was formed upon the bank of the river, and we began to climb the steep bluff that rose some two hundred feet above the water. Before the ascent was completed, we heard heavy firing up the river on our right, showing that those who crossed the river above us had encountered the enemy. With a desperate resolution to crush the rebellion, we scrambled to the top, and our line was quickly formed upon its crest. A dense forest was in our immediate front, the firing on our right had increased, and the roar of regular volleys of musketry came rolling down the river.

Gray forms were seen flitting among the trees before us, puffs of white smoke suddenly burst out from the forest, and the uncomfortable "zip, zip" of leaden messengers over our heads warned us that the enemy meant business. We returned the fire, and sent our first greetings to the Southern Confederacy, in the form of minie bullets, that went singing and cracking through the forest in our front; and we made a target of every gray form we could see.

Our regiment was about to make a charge upon them, when the order came for us to get down over the bluff, and recross the river as rapidly as possible, and down through the rocks and trees we ran. We reached the river, and began to make a most masterly advance upon Maryland. The enemy followed us to the top of the bluff, and would have punished us severely as we were recrossing the river, but one of our batteries went into position on the Maryland side, threw shells over our heads, and drove the rebels back. Several of the regiments on our right had sustained great losses; one of them, the 118th Pennsylvania, had been almost annihilated. Upon reaching the Maryland shore, we took possession of the Chesapeake and Ohio canal, and there formed the advanced line of the army.

One very amusing incident occurred in our retreat. In Company H was a man by the name of Tommy Welch, an Irishman about forty years of age, a brave, generous-hearted fellow. He was an old bachelor, and one of those funny, neat, particular men we occasionally meet. He always looked as if he had emerged from a bandbox; and the boys used to say that he would rather sacrifice the whole army of the Potomac, than to have a spot of rust upon his rifle, or dust upon his uniform. He was always making the most laughable blunders, and was usually behind all others in obeying any command. When our regiment went tumbling down over the side of the bluff, to reach the river, the men all got down before Tommy understood what they were doing. Then very slowly he descended, picking his path carefully among the trees and rocks, and did not reach the river until the rear of the regiment was nearly one-half of the way across. The officer who commanded our regiment on that day rode a magnificent horse, and as the regiment recrossed, he sat coolly upon his horse near the Virginia shore, amidst the shots of the enemy, speaking very pleasantly to the men as they passed him. He evidently determined to be the last man of the regiment to leave the post of danger. He saw Uncle Tommy, and although the danger was very great, he kindly waited for him to cross. When the latter reached the water, with great deliberation he sat down upon a rock, and removed his shoes and stockings, and slowly packed them away in his blanket. Then his pant legs must be rolled up, so that they would not come in contact with the water; and all the time the rebels were coming nearer, and the bullets were flying more thickly. At last he was ready for an advance movement, but just as he reached the water, the luckless pant legs slipped down over his knees, and he very quietly retraced his steps to the shore, to roll them up again. This was too much for even the courtesy of the commanding officer, who becoming impatient at the protracted delay, and not relishing the sound of the lead whistling over his head, cried out in a sharp voice: "Come, come, my man, hurry up, hurry up, or we will both be shot." Tommy looked up with that bewildered, serio-comic gravity of expression for which the Emerald Isle is so noted, and answered in the broadest brogue: "The divil a bit, sur. It is no mark of a gintleman to be in a hurry." The officer waited no longer, but putting spurs to his horse, he dashed across the river, while Tommy, carrying his rifle in one hand, and holding up his pant legs in the other, followed after, the bullets flying thickly around him.

At the Battle of the Wilderness, he and the 20th Maine fought desperately, until they were flanked and forced to fall back; but even in retreat they managed to gain some small victories...

Battle of the Wilderness (May 5-7, 1864).

The rebels evidently knew but little of our force, position and intention, and it is safe to say we knew less of theirs; and thus the two great masses of men were hurled against each other. The rebels fought like demons, and under cover of the dense underbrush poured deadly volleys upon us. The air was filled with lead. Minie bullets went snapping and tearing through the pine limbs; splinters flew in every direction; trees were completely riddled with bullets in a moment's time; blood ran in torrents; death lost its terror; and men for a time seemed transformed to beings that had no fear. Major Spear, aided by the field and line officers, gallantly led the regiment on. Our lines were broken. It was a disorganized battle; every man fought for himself and by himself, but all faced the enemy with heroic daring, and were determined that the tide of victory should set on the Union side. With remorseless determination the rebels poured their deadly fire upon our men, and they, with irresistible power, pressed back the foe. The rebels retreated across a small field that had been cleared in the heart of the great forest, and reforming their lines in the edge of the woods prepared to receive us. By this time our regiment had worked its way well up to the front line. General Bartlett, in person, led our brigade in its charge across the field. As we stood for a moment and looked upon that field, and saw where the bullets were falling into the dried soil, and the little clouds of dust arising so thickly, we were reminded of heavy drops of rain falling just before the shower comes in its full force.

The order was given to charge. The right of our regiment now rested upon the turnpike; and across the field we dashed. Zip, zip, zip, came the bullets on every side. The field was nearly crossed. We dashed up a little swell of land on its farthest side and were under the shadow of the trees. A red volcano yawned before us and vomited forth fire, and lead, and death. Our lines staggered for a moment, but with desperate resolution our men threw themselves upon the enemy's guns. It was not child's play, but more like a conflict of giants. North and South arrayed against each other, man against man. The sons of the Pine Tree State crossed bayonets with those who were reared under the orange groves of the far South. The rifle barrels touched, as from their muzzles they poured death into each other's faces; the ground shook with the roar of musketry; the forest trees were flaming with fire, and the air was loaded with death. Foot after foot the rebels retreated, their gray forms mantled with fire as they went. Slowly and steadily we advanced, giving blows with a mailed hand as we pursued the foe. What a medley of sounds, the incessant roar of the rifle; the screaming bullets; the forest on fire; men cheering, groaning, yelling, swearing, and praying! All this created an experience in the minds of the survivors that we can never forget.

The right of our regiment reached a small field, while our left was buried in the forest beyond. Major Spear ordered our colors to advance into the open field, and the regiment to form upon them; but just as this movement was being executed, we received a sharp and fatal volley from our right and rear. We at first supposed the brigade upon our right had mistaken us for the enemy, and had fired through mistake; but Major Spear was informed at that moment that the Sixth corps had failed to connect with our division, and consequently the brigade upon our right had fallen back, and the enemy was in our rear. Our only way of escape was by the left flank, while each man worked his way back to the breastworks. It was a very narrow escape for us, and it was only by a quick, daring dash that we escaped from the snare in which we found ourselves. The regiment regained the line of breastworks, losing heavily in killed and wounded, but capturing many prisoners. Company H entered the battle with thirty men, and came out with eighteen.

Many deeds of daring were done that day by members of our regiment, which, if all recorded, would fill a large volume. I will only mention a few that have come to my knowledge. Captain Walter G. Morrill, of Company B, discovering that the enemy was coming down upon our right flank, marshaled a fragment of his own company, and a few men from other commands, formed a little line of battle along the turnpike, and for some minutes held a large force of the rebels in check. It is doubtful if the brave captain would have retreated at all, if a minie-ball had not gone crashing through his face, and hurled him to the ground. Regaining his feet, he bound a handkerchief around his face, and continued to fight until he was blinded and choked with blood, when his brave men assisted him to the rear.

...

Lieutenant Melcher, whose company was the left of our regiment, did not learn that we were flanked, and with a small squad of men continued to advance until he discovered that the firing was all in his rear. Then he went out on the turnpike and looked in the direction of the breastworks, and saw a line of rebel infantry stretched across the road behind him. He went back to his men, told them of the situation, and mustered his force. He found that he had fifteen men, among whom were Sergeants Smith, of Company F, and Rogers, of Company H. A council of war was held. They must decide to do one of three things: continue to advance and capture Richmond; remain where they were and be taken prisoners ; or cut their way through the rebel line of battle and rejoin their regiment at the breastworks. Not a single man would listen to the thought of surrender. Some, I think, would have dared to make the advance upon Richmond. It was finally decided to cut their way through the enemy's line, and escape. It was a dangerous undertaking, but they were men who dared to face danger and death. With loaded rifles and fixed bayonets they moved with noiseless tread toward the rebel line. They were guided by the firing, which, however, had much abated, and soon through the pine trees they caught a glimpse of the rebels. With a yell the little band charged upon a force that could have brought a regiment to contend with each man in that little squad. There was a flash and a roar. Melcher's voice was heard calling upon them to surrender. The rebels, of course, were surprised, and their line was broken and divided. The squad of fifteen lost two or three men in the shock, but swept on to our line of battle, bearing with them thirty prisoners, which they had torn from the rebel line in their mad charge.

During the Siege of Petersburg, our young hero and his friends had their mealtime interrupted by a Confederate mortar...

The campaign became quite scientific, so that after the first few weeks, we learned to tell by the sound the nature of every missile that passed over us, and knew just which ones to dodge. Of course the mortar shells had the most terror for us. The ordinary field-pieces or siege-guns, that threw shells directly through the air, did not disturb us much, as we lay behind our breastworks, but those confounded mortars, throwing those enormous shells up in almost a perpendicular direction, with such a peculiar aim that, when they reached a certain degree of altitude, they would descend plump within our lines, tearing up the earth in a most frightful manner, and filling the air with death-dealing missiles by their terrible explosions, so that our only safety was in the bomb-proofs. We always told short stories when we heard them coming. As we became accustomed to the new situation in which we found ourselves, we learned to take all the advantages of it we possibly could. The bomb-proofs of course were damp and unhealthy, so we had our tents out in the open air, and fled to the bomb-proofs when danger threatened us. We also built dining pavilions, in which we used to eat. These were not very elaborate edifices, but answered their purpose; a few pieces of shelter tent were spread upon short posts, to protect us from the hot rays of the sun, the sides were left open to allow a circulation of air, a rough table and benches were constructed, and under those shelters we would dine in what, to us at least, was a metropolitan style. But how often would those meals be interrupted in the most abrupt and amusing manner! We will relate one instance. It is one o'clock in the afternoon of a hot, sweltering day; the enemy has been shelling us in a most vigorous manner all the forenoon; an agent of the sanitary commission has made us a visit, leaving us potatoes, onions, soft bread, pickles, and a few other luxuries, and the event must be commemorated by a good square dinner. In the inspiration of the preparation we forgot Lee's army, the dreaded mortar shells and all else, and our feast is soon spread upon the table in our dining pavilion, while six rough, unshaved, sunburned fellows place their legs beneath the table, and prepare to devour the rations that have been dealt out to their mess. They are a happy squad; they talk and laugh in high glee. The preliminaries on those occasions were very brief, and the food is quickly deposited within the plates of the hungry fellows, but just at that moment a noise that is utterly indescribable fills the air; it is a medley of shuddering, shrieking, agonizing groans, as if the air was alive with demons, uttering their most demoniac yells with an infinite power an incarnate hell that is descending upon us with lightning speed. The boys understand what it is; rules of etiquette are forgotten, and each voice utters those dreaded words, a shell, a shell, and six men charge for the bomb-proof. In their hasty departure Horton came in contact with one of the four posts that supported the roof of the pavilion, and down came the structure. Unfortunately for Wyman, the table was between him and the bombproof, and as he sprang over the former to reach the latter, his foot caught in the table somewhere, and as a result of the accident he entered the bomb-proof upon his head and shoulders, leaving the path along which he came strewn with potatoes, onions, and other articles in the culinary department. The dinner was almost a failure, and what rendered the circumstance more aggravating to the parties so directly interested, was the fact that the shell did not strike within several rods of them, and would not have done them any harm if they had remained at their table.

Finally, at the Battle of Five Forks, Theodore and his companions were forced to fall back in the face of overwhelming fire; but while they were falling back, they encountered a young man who didn't approve of their retreat...

It was now past noon. Heavy firing was heard on our right, both musketry and artillery. It was but a short distance from us, and we knew that our division had encountered the enemy. For an hour we listened with much anxiety, and then the order came for us to advance. We crossed the field, and found the rebels in the woods, on the other side. The roar of battle on our right inspired us, and we rushed upon them. They gave us a heavy skirmish fire, and then fell back for a half mile, we following them very closely. Suddenly there was a sheet of flame in our front. Whiz, crash, bang, went a dozen shells above our heads. We had reached the enemy's line of battle, and a heavy infantry fire was also opened upon us. It was of course impossible to advance further. It would be folly to remain where we were, and so we fell rapidly back.

Many of our men were wounded before we got out of the range of the enemy's guns. One, a brave young fellow from Massachusetts, fell, shot through both legs. We would not leave him in the hands of the rebels, and laid him upon a blanket, to carry him back. He was much excited, and was determined not to be carried off the field. He called us miserable cowards for falling back from the enemy, and pleaded with us to put him down, and with our little skirmish line, charge upon the rebels' line of battle.

CHAPTER NINE

*THE ROOM IS TOO SMALL FOR EVEN A WOMAN TO
MISS SIX TIMES*

— PHOEBE PEMBER —

*P*hoebe Pember was born into wealth and privilege in Charleston, South Carolina, as Phoebe Levy in 1823. She was the daughter of successful merchant Jacob Levy and prominent actress Phoebe Yates. She was married in 1856 to Thomas Pember, but he died soon after their marriage, and by the time war broke out, she was living with her parents in Georgia.

In 1862, she was asked to consider serving as a matron at one of the Army hospitals in Richmond, Virginia. She accepted the position, and in December she became the matron of Chimborazo Hospital on the western outskirts of Richmond. This was no trifling assignment, Chimborazo was the largest military hospital in the world during the 1860s, and Phoebe was the first woman to hold any position at the hospital.

As part of her duties, she was in charge of the preparation and administration of the medicine and special diets prescribed by the hospital's surgeons. She also took time to personally read for, write for, and otherwise give special attention to as many wounded men as she possibly could. It is estimated that around 15,000 men came under her care during the course of the war. During her service, Phoebe *had many interesting experiences; here are a few of her most interesting stories*[14]...

The First Day

When Phoebe accepted the position, she had no real idea of her duties or powers, and really didn't know what she was in for. Her first day started with a meeting with the surgeon-in-charge at Chimborazo...

He was a cultivated, gentlemanly man, kind-hearted when he remembered to be so, and very much afraid of any responsibility resting upon his shoulders. No prepara-

Phoebe Pember, in 1855.

tions had been made by him for his female department. He escorted me into a long, low, whitewashed building, open from end to end, called for two benches, and then, with entire composure, as if surrounding circumstances were most favorable, commenced an aesthetic conversation on belles letters, female influence, and the first, last and only novel published during the war. (It was a translation of Joseph the Second, printed on gray and bound in marbled wall-paper.) A neat compliment offered at leave-taking rounded off the interview, with a parting promise from him to send me the carpenter to

---

[14] Taken from *A Southern Woman's Story*, by Phoebe Yates Pember, 1879.

make partitions and shelves for office, parlor, laundry, pantry and kitchen. The steward was then summoned for consultation, and my representative reign began.

A stove was unearthed; very small, very rusty, and fit only for a family of six. There were then about six hundred men upon the matron's diet list, the illest ones to be supplied with food from my kitchen, and the convalescents from the steward's, called, in contra-distinction from mine, "the big kitchen." Just then my mind could hardly grope through the darkness that clouded it, as to what were my special duties, but one mental spectrum always presented itself— *chicken soup.*

Having vaguely heard of requisitions, I then and there made my first, in very unofficial style. A polite request sent through "Jim" (a small black boy) to the steward for a pair of chickens. They came instantly ready dressed for cooking. Jim picked up some shavings, kindled up the stove, begged, borrowed or stole (either act being lawful to his mind), a large iron pot from the big kitchen. For the first time I cut up with averted eyes a raw bird, and the Rubicon was passed.

My readers must not suppose that this picture applies generally to all our hospitals, or that means and appliances so early in the war for food and comfort, were so meagre. This state of affairs was only the result of accident and some misunderstanding. The surgeon of my hospital naturally thought I had informed myself of the power vested in me by virtue of my position, and, having some experience, would use the rights given me by the law passed in Congress, to arrange my own department; and I, on reading the bill, could only understand that the office was one that dovetailed the duties of housekeeper and cook, nothing more.

In the meantime the soup was boiling, and was undeniably a success, from the perfume it exhaled. Nature may not have intended me for a Florence Nightingale, but a kitchen proved my worth. Frying-pans, griddles, stew-pans and coffee-pots soon became my household gods. The niches must have been prepared years previously, invisible to the naked eye but still there.

Gaining courage from familiarity with my position, a venture across the lane brought me to the nearest ward (they were all separate buildings, it must be remembered, covering a half mile of ground in a circle, one story high, with long, low windows opening back in a groove against the inside wall), and, under the first I peeped in, lay the shadow of a man extended on his bed, pale and attennuated.

What woman's heart would not melt and make itself a home where so much needed?

His wants were inquired into, and, like all the humbler class of men, who think that unless they have been living on hog and hominy they are starved, he complained of not having eaten anything "for three mortal weeks."

In the present state of the kitchen larder, there was certainly not much of a choice, and I was as yet ignorant of the capabilities of the steward's department. However, soup was suggested, as a great soother of "misery in his back," and a generous supply of adjectives prefixed for flavor—"nice, hot, good chicken soup." The suggestion was received kindly. If it was very nice he would take some: "he was never, though, much of a hand for drinks." My mind rejected the application of words, but matter not mind, was the subject under consideration.

All my gastronomic experience revolted against soup without the sick man's parsley; and Jim, my acting partner, volunteered to get some at a mysterious place he always called "The Dutchman's," so at last, armed with a bowl full of the decoction, duly salted, peppered, and seasoned, I again sought my first patient.

He rose deliberately—so deliberately that I felt sensible of the great favor he was conferring. He smoothed his tangled locks with a weak hand, took a piece of well-masticated tobacco from between three or four solitary teeth, but still the soup was unappropriated, and it appeared evident that some other preliminaries were to be arranged. The novelty of my position, added to a lively imagination, suggested fears that he might think it necessary to arise for compliment's sake; and hospital clothing being made to suit the scarcity and expense of homespun, the idea was startling. But my suspense did not continue long; he was only seeking for a brown-covered tract hid under his pillow.

Did he intend to read grace before meat? No, he simply wanted a pocket-handkerchief, which cruel war had denied; so without comment a leaf was quietly abstracted and used for that purpose. The result was satisfactory, for the next moment the bowl was taken from my hand, and the first spoonful of soup transmitted to his mouth.

It was an awful minute! My fate seemed to hang upon the fiat of that uneducated palate. A long painful gulp, a "judgmatical" shake of the head, not in the affirmative, and the bowl traveled slowly back to my extended hand.

"My mammy's soup was not like that," he whined. "But I might worry a little down if it wasn't for them weeds a-floating round."

Well! why be depressed? There may not after all be any actual difference between weed's and herbs.

After that first day improvements rapidly progressed. Better stoves, and plenty of them, were put up; closets enclosed; china or its substitutes, pottery and tin, supplied. I learned to make requisitions and to use my power. The coffee, tea, milk, and all other luxuries provided for the sick wards, were, through my demand, turned over to me...

Still my office did not rise above that of chief cook, for I dared not leave my kitchen unattended for a moment, till Dr. M., one day, passing the window, and seeing me seated on a low bench peeling potatoes, appeared much surprised, and inquired where my cooks were. Explanations followed, a copy of hospital rules were sent for, and authority found to provide the matron's department with suitable attendants. A gentle, sweet-tempered lady, extremely neat and efficient, was appointed assistant matron, also three or four cooks and bakers.

Writing A Letter

Many soldiers were either illiterate, or too sickly to write their own letters. Therefore, Phoebe wrote many letters for many soldiers who wished to send news of their condition to friends and loved ones. Sometimes the results were most impressive.

"Kin you writ me a letter?" drawled a whining voice from a bed in one of the wards, a cold day in '62.

The speaker was an up-country Georgian, one of the kind called "Goubers" by the soldiers generally; lean, yellow, attenuated, with wispy strands of hair hanging over his high, thin cheek-bones. He put out a hand to detain me and the nails were like claws.

"Why do you not let the nurse cut your nails?"

"Because I aren't got any spoon, and I use them instead."

"Will you let me have your hair cut, then? You can't get well with all that dirty hair hanging about your eyes and ears."

"No, I can't git my hair cut, kase as how I promised my mammy that I would let it grow till the war be over. Oh, it's onlucky to cut it!"

"Then I can't write any letter for you. Do what I wish you to do, and then I will oblige you."

This was plain talking. The hair was cut (I left the nails for another day), my portfolio brought, and sitting by the side of his bed I waited for further orders. They came with a formal introduction, — "for Mrs. Marthy Brown."

"My dear Mammy:

"I hope this finds you well, as it leaves me well, and I hope that I shall git a furlough Christmas, and come and see you, and I hope that you will keep well, and all the folks be well by that time, as I hopes to be well myself. This leaves me in good health, as I hope it finds you and"

But here I paused, as his mind seemed to be going round in a circle, and asked him a few questions about his home, his position during the last summer's campaign, how he got sick, and where his brigade was at that time. Thus furnished with some material to work upon, the latter proceeded rapidly. Four sides were conscientiously filled, for no soldier would think a letter worth sending home that showed any blank paper. Transcribing his name, the number of his ward and proper address, so that an answer might reach him — the composition was read to him. Gradually his pale face brightened, a sitting posture was assumed with difficulty (for, in spite of his determined effort in his letter "to be well," he was far from convalescence). As I folded and directed it, contributed the expected five-cent stamp, and handed it to him, he gazed cautiously around to be sure there were no listeners.

"Did you writ all that?" he asked, whispering, but with great emphasis.

"Yes."

"Did I say all that?"

"I think you did."

A long pause of undoubted admiration — astonishment ensued.

Hiring Some Help

Eventually, Phoebe decided that she needed more help. So, she set out to hire some steady assistants; but unfortunately, everything did not go according to plan...

The wounded men at this time began to make serious complaints that the liquor issued did not reach them, and no vigilance on my part appeared to check the improper appropriation of it, or lead to any discovery of the thieves in the wards. There were many obstacles to be surmounted before proper precautions could be taken. Lumber was so expensive that closets in each ward were out of the question, and if made locks could not be purchased for any amount of money. The liquor, therefore, when it left my quarters, was open to any passer-by in the wards who would watch his opportunity; so, although I had strong and good reasons for excluding female nurses, the supposition that liquor would be no temptation to them, and would be more apt to reach its proper destination through their care, determined me to engage them.

Unlucky thought, born in an evil hour!

There were no lack of applications when the want was circulated, but my choice hesitated between ladies of education and position, who I knew would be willing to aid me, and the common class of respectable servants. The latter suited best, because it was to be supposed they would be more amenable to authority. They were engaged, and the very sick wards divided among three of them. They were to keep the bed-clothing in order, receive and dispense the liquor, carry any delicacy in the way of food where it was most needed, and in fact do anything reasonable that was requested. The next day my new corps were in attendance, and the different liquors, beverages and stimulants delivered to them under the black looks of the ward-masters. No. 1 received hers silently. She was a cross-looking woman from North Carolina, painfully ugly, or rather what is termed hard-featured, and apparently very taciturn; the last quality rather an advantage. She had hardly left my kitchen when she returned with all the drinks, and a very indignant face.

In reply to inquiries made she proved her taciturnity was not chronic. She asserted loudly that she was a decent woman, and "was not going anywhere in a place where a man sat up on his bed in his shirt, and the rest laughed — she knew they were laughing at her." The good old proverb that talking is silver but silence is gold had impressed itself on my mind long before this, so I silently took her charge from her, telling her that a hospital was no place for a person of her delicate sensibilities, and at the same time holding up Miss G. and myself (who were young enough to be her daughters), as examples for her imitation.

She answered truly that we acted as we pleased and so would she; and that was the last I saw of her. What her ideas of hospital life were I never inquired, and shall never know.

No. 2 came briskly forward. She was a plausible, light-haired, light-eyed and light-complexioned Englishwoman; very petite, with a high nose. She had come to the hospital with seven trunks, which ought to have been a warning to me, but she brought such strong recommendations from responsible parties that they warped my judgment. She received the last trust handed her — an open pitcher of hot punch — with averted head, nose turned aside, and held it at arm's length with a high disdain mounted upon her high nose. Her excuse for this antipathy was that the smell of liquor was "awful," she "could not a-bear it," and "it turned her witals." This was rather suspicious, but we deferred judgment.

Dinner was distributed. No. 2 appeared, composed, vigilant and attentive to her duties, carrying her delicacies of food to her wards with the assistance of the nurses. No. 3, an inoffensive woman did the same, and all worked well. That afternoon, when I had retired to my little sanctum to take the one hour's rest that I allowed myself each day undisturbed, Miss G. put her head in the door with an apprehensive look and said, "the new matrons wished to see me." They were admitted, and my high-nosed friend, who had been elected spokeswoman it seems, said after a few preliminaries, with a toss of her head and a couple of sniffs that I "seemed to have made myself very comfortable."

This was assented to graciously. She added that other people were not, who were quite as much entitled to style. This also remained undisputed, and then she stated her real grievance, that they "were not satisfied, for I had not invited them to call upon me, or into my room," and "they considered themselves quite as much ladies as I was." I answered I was glad to hear it, and hoped they would always act as ladies should, and in a way suitable to the title. There was an evident desire on her part to say more, but she had not calculated up-on the style of reception, and therefore was thrown out beyond her line of action, so she civilly requested me to call and inspect their quarters that they were dissatisfied with. An hour later I did so, and found them sitting around a sociable spittoon, with a friendly box of snuff — dipping! I found it impossible to persuade them that the government was alone responsible for their poor quarters, they persisted in holding me answerable.

The next day, walking through one of the wards under No. 2's charge, I found a part of the building, of about eight to ten feet square, portioned off, a roughly improvised plank partition dividing this temporary room from the rest of the ward. Seated comfortably therein was the new matron, entrenched among her trunks. A neat table and comfortable chair, abstracted from my few kitchen appurtenances, added to her comforts. Choice pieces of crockery, remnants of more luxurious times, that had at one time adorned my shelves, were disposed tastefully around, and the drinks issued by me for the patients were conveniently placed at her elbow. She explained that she kept them there to prevent thefts. Perhaps the nausea communicated from their neighborhood had tinted the high nose higher, and there was a defiant look about her, as if she sniffed the battle afar.

It was very near though, and had to be fought, however disagreeable, so I instantly entered into explanations, short, but polite. Each patient being allowed, by law, a certain number of feet, every inch taken therefrom was so much ventilation lost, and the abstraction of as much space as she had taken for illegal purposes was a serious matter, and conflicted with the rules that governed the hospital. Besides this, no woman was allowed to stay in the wards, for obvious reasons. No. 2, however, was a sensible person, for she did not waste her breath in talking; she merely held her position. An appeal made by me to the surgeon of the ward did not result favorably; he said I had engaged her, she belonged to my corps, and was under my supervision: so I sent for the steward.

The steward of a hospital cannot define exactly what his duties are, the difficulty being to find out what they are not. Whenever it has to be decided who has to fill a disagreeable office, the choice invariably falls upon the steward. So a message was sent to his quarters to request him to compel No. 2 to evacuate her hastily improvised premises. He hesitated long, but engaging at last the services of his assistant, a broad-shouldered fighting character, proceeded to eject the new tenant.

He commenced operations by polite explanations; but they were met in a startling manner. She arose and rolled up her sleeves, advancing upon him as he receded down the ward. The sick and wounded men roared with laughter, cheering her on, and she remained mistress of the field. Dinner preparations served as an interlude and silently suppressed, she as usual made her entree into the kitchen, received the drinks for her ward and vanished. Half an hour elapsed and then the master of the ward in which she had domiciled herself made his report to me, and recounted a pitiful tale. He was a neat quiet manager, and usually kept his quarters beautifully clean. No. 2, he said, divided the dinner, and whenever she came across a bone in hash or stew, or indeed anything therein displeased her, she took it in her fingers and dashed it upon the floor. With so little to make a hospital gay, this peculiar epi-

sode was a god-send to the soldiers, and indeed to all the look-
ers on. The surgeons stood laughing, in groups, the men
crowded to the windows of the belligerent power, and a *coup-
d'état* became necessary.

"Send me the carpenter!" I felt the spirit of Boadicea. The
man stepped up; he had always been quiet, civil and obedient.

"Come with me into Ward E."

A few steps took us there.

"Knock down that partition and carry away those boards."
It was *un fait accompli.*

But the victory was not gained, only the fortifications
stormed and taken, for almost hidden by flying splinters and
dust, No. 2 sat among her seven trunks enthroned like Rome
upon her seven hills.

The story furnishes no further interest, but the result was
very annoying. She was put into my ambulance very drunk by
this time and sent away, her trunks sent after her. The next
day, neatly dressed, she managed to get an interview with the
medical director, enlisted his sympathy by a plausible appeal
and description of her desolate condition. "A refugee," or
"refewgee," as she called herself, "trying to make her living
decently," and receiving an order to report at our hospital, was
back there by noon. Explanations had to be written, and our
surgeon-in-chief to interfere with his authority, before we
could get rid of her.

The Whiskey Barrel

*Finding that much of the whiskey she was supposed to distribute
was disappearing before it ever reached her, our heroine set out to
gain complete control of all the "medicinal" liquor.*

Daily inspection too, convinced me that great evils still existed under my rule, in spite of my zealous care for my patients. For example, the monthly barrel of whiskey which I
was entitled to draw still remained at the dispensary under the
guardianship of the apothecary and his clerks, and quarts and
pints were issued through any order coming from surgeons or
their substitutes, so that the contents were apt to be gone long
before I was entitled to draw more, and my sick would suffer
for want of the stimulant. There were many suspicious circumstances connected with this *institution*; for the monthly
barrel was an institution and a very important one. Indeed, if
it is necessary to have a hero for this matter-of-fact narrative
the whiskey barrel will have to step forward and make his
bow.

So again I referred to the hospital bill passed by Congress,
which provided that liquors in common with other luxuries,
belonged to the matron's department, and in an evil moment,
such an impulse as tempted Pandora to open the fatal casket
assailed me, and I despatched the bill, flanked by a formal requisition for the liquor. An answer came in the shape of the
head surgeon. He declared I would find "the charge most on-
erous," that "whiskey was required at all hours, sometimes in
the middle of the night, and even if I remained at the hospital,
he would not like me to be disturbed," "it was constantly
needed for medicinal purposes," "he was responsible for its
proper application;" but I was not convinced, and withstood
all argument and persuasion. He was proverbially sober himself, but I was aware why both commissioned and non-
commissioned officers opposed violently the removal of the
liquor to my quarters. So, the printed law being at hand for

reference, I nailed my colors to the mast, and that evening all the liquor was in my pantry and the key in my pocket.

...despite continued bickering by those who no longer had access to their "medicine," Phoebe remained steadfast, and her patients received their doses with more regularity.

This was not the end of the story however. When Lee's Army evacuated Richmond in April 1865, she was left in charge of the Hospital with no guards or other military protection. Soon, some folks came looking for what they felt was rightfully theirs...

Exhausted with all the exciting events of the day, it was not to be wondered at that I soon fell asleep heavily and dreamlessly, to be awakened in an hour by the crash of an adjoining door, and passing into my pantry from whence the sound proceeded I came upon a group of men, who had burst the entrance opening upon the back premises. As my eye traveled from face to face, I recognized them as a set of "hospital rats" whom I had never been able to get rid of, for if sent to the field one week, they would be sure to be back the next, on some trifling pretext of sickness or disability. The ringleader was an old enemy, who had stored up many a grievance against me, but my acts of kindness to his sickly wife naturally made me suppose his wrath had been disarmed. He acted on this occasion as spokesman, and the trouble was the old one. Thirty gallons of whiskey had been sent to me the day before the evacuation, and they wanted it.

"We have come for the whiskey!"

"You cannot, and shall not have it."

"It does not belong to you."

"It is in my charge, and I intend to keep it. Go out of my pantry; you are all drunk."

"Boys!" he said, "pick up that barrel and carry it down the hill. I will attend to her!"

But the habit of obedience of four years still had its effect on the boys, for all the movement they made was in a retrograde direction.

"Wilson," I said, "you have been in this hospital a long time. Do you think from what you know of me that the whiskey can be taken without my consent?"

He became very insolent.

"Stop that talk; your great friends have all gone, and we won't stand that now. Move out of the way!"

He advanced towards the barrel, and so did I, only being in the inside, I interposed between him and the object of contention. The fierce temper blazed up in his face, and catching me roughly by the shoulder, he called me a name that a decent woman seldom hears and even a wicked one resents.

But I had a little friend, which usually reposed quietly on the shelf, but had been removed to my pocket in the last twenty-four hours, more from a sense of protection than from any idea that it would be called into active service; so before he had time to push me one inch from my position, or to see what kind of an ally was in my hand, that sharp click, a sound so significant and so different from any other, struck upon his ear, and sent him back amidst his friends, pale and shaken.

"You had better leave," I said, composedly (for I felt in my feminine soul that although I was near enough to pinch his nose, that I had missed him), "for if one bullet is lost, there are five more ready, and the room is too small for even a woman to miss six times."

There was a conference held at the shattered door, resulting in an agreement to leave, but he shook his fist wrathfully at my small pop-gun.

"You think yourself very brave now, but wait an hour; perhaps others may have pistols too, and you won't have it entirely your way after all."

My first act was to take the head of one of the flour barrels and nail it across the door as tightly as I could, with a two-pound weight for a hammer, and then, warm with triumph and victory gained, I sat down by my whiskey barrel and felt the affection we all bestow on what we have cherished, fought for, and defended successfully; then putting a candle, a box of matches, and a pistol within reach of my hand, I went to sleep, never waking until late in the morning, having heard nothing more of my visitors.

Union Occupation

Finally, the Union Army occupied Richmond and took over the hospitals. Phoebe stayed on until there were no more soldiers to be cared for, and through it all she continued to fearlessly do all she could to make sure those under her care had their needs properly supplied.

...the steward informed me that our stores had been taken possession of by the Federal authorities, so we could not draw the necessary' rations. The surgeons had all left; therefore I prepared for a visit to headquarters, by donning my full-dress toilette: boots of untanned leather, tied with thongs'; a Georgia woven homespun dress in black and white blocks — the white, cotton yarn, the black, an old silk, washed, scraped with broken glass into pulp, and then carded and spun (it was an elegant thing); white cuffs and collar of bleached homespun, and a hat plaited of the rye straw picked from the field back of us, dyed black with walnut juice, a shoe-string for ribbon to encircle it; and knitted worsted gloves of three shades of green—the darkest bottle shade being around the wrist, while the color tapered to the loveliest blossom of the pea at the finger-tips. The style of the make was Confederate.

Thus splendidly equipped I walked to Dr. M.'s office, now Federal headquarters, and making my way through a crowd of blue coats, accosted the principal figure seated there, with a stern and warlike demand for food, and a curt inquiry whether it was their intention to starve their captured sick. He was very polite, laid the blame on the obstructions in the river, which prevented their transports getting up. I requested that as such was the case I might be allowed to reclaim my ambulance, now under their lock and key, in order to take some coffee then in my possession to the city and exchange it for animal food. It had been saved from rations formerly drawn, and donations given. He wished to know why it had not been turned over to the U. S. government, but did not press the point as I was not communicative, and gave me the necessary order for the vehicle. Then polite conversation commenced.

"Was I a native of Virginia?"

"No; I was a South Carolinian, who had gone to Virginia at the commencement of the war to try and aid in alleviating the sufferings and privations of the hospitals."

"He had lost a brother in South Carolina."

"It was the fate of war. Self-preservation was the first law of nature. As a soldier he must recognize defense of one's native soil."

...

But his kindness had once again put my ambulance under my control, and placing a bag of coffee and a demijohn of whiskey in it, I assumed the reins, having no driver, and went to market. The expedition was successful, as I returned shortly with a live calf, for which I had exchanged them, and which summoned everyone within hearing by its bellowing. I had quite won the heart of the Vermonter who had been sentry at my door, and though patriotic souls may not believe me, he paid me many compliments at the expense of the granite ladies of his State. The compliments were sincere, as he refused the drink of whiskey my gratitude offered him.

My next visit was to the commissary department of my hospital in search of sugar. Two Federal guards were in charge, but they simply stared with astonishment as I put aside their bayonets and unlocked the door of the place with my pass-key, filled my basket, with an explanation to them that I could be arrested whenever wanted at my quarters.

After this no one opposed my erratic movements, the newcomers ignoring me. No explanation was ever given to me, why I was allowed to come and go, nurse my men and feed them with all I could take or steal. All I ever gathered was from one of our errand-boys, who had fraternized with a Yankee sutler, who told him confidentially that the Federal surgeon in charge thought that woman in black had better go home, and added on his own responsibility, "He's awful afraid of her."

Away I was compelled to go at last, for my sick were removed to another hospital, where I still attended to them. There congregated the ladies of the neighborhood, bringing what delicacies they could gather, and nursing indiscriminately any patient who needed care. This continued till all the sick were either convalescent or dead, and at last my vocation was gone, and not one invalid left to give me a pretext for daily occupation.

CHAPTER TEN

THE FALLING FLAG

— APPOMATTOX COURT HOUSE —

O n April 9, 1865, General Robert E. Lee surrendered his Army of Northern Virginia to Union General Ulysses S. Grant. This essentially ended the Civil War. The next month would see the surrender of most of the rest of the forces of the Confederacy, and there would be no more major battles.

Here we find a truly interesting coincidence and one of the unique stories of the Civil War. The two Generals met in the parlor of a home in the small town of Appomattox Court House, Virginia. The home was owned by Wilmer McLean. The first major battle of the Civil War (the Battle of Bull Run, or Manassas) took place on and around Mr. McLean's farm at Manassas, Virginia, with an artillery round coming down the chimney into his kitchen fireplace.

He then moved his family to Appomattox Court House, in southern Virginia so they would be farther from the fighting; but the war found its way back into his home on the fateful morning of April 9th. It is said that Mr. McLean was fond of telling people that the war began in his front yard and ended in his parlor.

Mr. McLean's story is certainly unique, but there were many other interesting stories which took place surrounding Lee's surrender. Here are the stories of some of the men who found themselves caught up in the important events of that day.

A Final Act Of Respect

John Brown Gordon commanded the final attack of Lee's Army on the morning of April 9th. He attempted to break out and create an escape for the surrounded Army, but his attempt failed, and Lee was forced to surrender the Army. When he received Gordon's message that he had been unable to break out, General Lee responded by saying, "Then there is nothing left for me to do but to go and see General Grant and I would rather die a thousand deaths."

A few days after Lee and Grant had agreed to the surrender, the Confederate's stacked their arms and surrendered them to the victorious Union command. General Gordon recounts[15] his experience of the ceremonial surrender of his command...

As my command, in worn-out shoes and ragged uniforms, but with proud mien, moved to the designated point to stack their arms and surrender their cherished battle-flags, they challenged the admiration of the brave victors. One of the knightliest soldiers of the Federal army, General Joshua L. Chamberlain of Maine, who afterward served with distinction as governor of his State, called his troops into line, and as my men marched in front of them, the veterans in blue gave a soldierly salute to those vanquished heroes--a token of respect from Americans to Americans, a final and fitting tribute from Northern to Southern chivalry.

General Chamberlain describes this incident in the following words:

---

[15] Taken from *Reminiscences of the Civil War*, by John B. Gordon, 1904.

At the sound of that machine-like snap of arms, General Gordon started, caught in a moment its significance, and instantly assumed the finest attitude of a soldier. He wheeled his horse, facing me, touching him gently with the spur, so that the animal slightly reared, and, as he wheeled, horse and rider made one motion, the horse's head swung down with a graceful bow, and General Gordon dropped his sword-point to his toe in salutation.

By word of mouth the general sent back orders to the rear that his own troops take the same position of the manual in the march past as did our line. That was done, and a truly imposing sight was the mutual salutation and farewell.

Bayonets were affixed to muskets, arms stacked, and cartridge-boxes unslung and hung upon the stacks. Then, slowly and with a reluctance that was appealingly pathetic, the torn and tattered battle-flags were either leaned against the stacks or laid upon the ground. The emotion of the conquered soldiery was really sad to witness. Some of the men who had carried and followed those ragged standards through the four long years of strife rushed, regardless of all discipline, from the ranks, bent about their old flags, and pressed them to their lips.

And it can well be imagined, too, that there was no lack of emotion on our side, but the Union men were held steady in their lines, without the least show of demonstration by word or by motion. There was, though, a twitching of the muscles of their faces, and, be it said, their battle-bronzed cheeks were not altogether dry. Our men felt the import of the occasion, and realized fully how they would have been affected if defeat and surrender had been their lot after such a fearful struggle.

(New York Times, May 4, 1901)

When the proud and sensitive sons of Dixie came to a full realization of the truth that the Confederacy was overthrown and their leader had been compelled to surrender his once invincible army, they could no longer control their emotions, and tears ran like water down their shrunken faces. The flags which they still carried were objects of undisguised affection. These Southern banners had gone down before overwhelming numbers; and torn by shells, riddled by bullets, and laden with the powder and smoke of battle, they aroused intense emotion in the men who had so often followed them to victory. Yielding to overpowering sentiment, these high-mettled men began to tear the flags from the staffs and hide them in their bosoms, as they wet them with burning tears.

The Confederate officers faithfully endeavored to check this exhibition of loyalty and love for the old flags. A great majority of them were duly surrendered; but many were secretly carried by devoted veterans to their homes, and will be cherished forever as honored heirlooms.

There was nothing unnatural or censurable in all this. The Confederates who clung to those pieces of battered bunting knew they would never again wave as martial ensigns above embattled hosts; but they wanted to keep them, just as they wanted to keep the old canteen with a bullet-hole through it, or the rusty gray jacket that had been torn by canister. They loved those flags, and will love them forever, as mementoes of the unparalleled struggle. They cherish them because they represent the consecration and courage not only of Lee's army but of all the Southern armies, because they symbolize the bloodshed and the glory of nearly a thousand battles.

The Final Charge

Alanson Randol was a Colonel of Cavalry in the 2nd Regiment of New York Cavalry, and this is his account[16] of the confusion surrounding the truce and surrender.

...we knew that we had them this time, and that at last Lee's proud army of Northern Virginia was at our mercy. While moving at almost a charging gait we were suddenly brought to a halt by reports of a surrender. General Sheridan and his staff rode up, and left in hot haste for the Court House; but just after leaving us, they were fired into by a party of rebel cavalry, who also opened fire on us, to which we promptly replied, and soon put them to flight. Our lines were then formed for a charge on the rebel infantry; but while the bugles were sounding the charge, an officer with a white flag rode out from the rebel lines, and we halted. It was fortunate for us that we halted when we did, for had we charged we would have been swept into eternity, as directly in our front was a creek, on the other side of which was a rebel brigade, entrenched, with batteries in position, the guns double shotted with canister. To have charged this formidable array, mounted, would have resulted in almost total annihilation. After we had halted, we were informed that preliminaries were being arranged for the surrender of Lee's whole army. At this news, cheer after cheer rent the air for a few moments, when soon all became as quiet as if nothing unusual had occurred. I rode forward between the lines with Custer and Pennington, and met several old friends among the rebels, who came out to see us. Among them, I remember Lee (Gimlet), of Virginia, and Cowan, of North Carolina. I saw General Cadmus Wilcox just

---

[16] Taken from *Last Days of the Rebellion*, by Alanson M. Randol, 1886.

across the creek, walking to and fro with his eyes on the ground, just as was his wont when he was instructor at West Point. I called to him, but he paid no attention, except to glance at me in a hostile manner.

While we were thus discussing the probable terms of the surrender, General Lee, in full uniform, accompanied by one of his staff, and General Babcock, of General Grant's staff, rode from the Court House towards our lines. As he passed us, we all raised our caps in salute, which he gracefully returned.

Later in the day loud and continuous cheering was heard among the rebels, which was taken up and echoed by our lines until the air was rent with cheers, when all as suddenly subsided. The surrender was a fixed fact, and the rebels were overjoyed at the very liberal terms they had received. Our men, without arms, approached the rebel lines, and divided their rations with the half-starved foe, and engaged in quiet, friendly conversation. There was no bluster nor braggadocia, — nothing but quiet contentment that the rebellion was crushed, and the war ended. In fact, many of the rebels seemed as much pleased as we were. Now and then one would meet a surly, dissatisfied look; but, as a general thing, we met smiling faces and hands eager and ready to grasp our own, especially if they contained anything to eat or drink. After the surrender, I rode over to the Court House with Colonel Pennington and others and visited the house in which the surrender had taken place, in search of some memento of the occasion. We found that everything had been appropriated before our arrival. Mr. Wilmer McLean, in whose house the surrender took place, informed us that on his farm at Manassas the first battle of Bull Run was fought. I asked him to write his name in my diary, for which, much to his surprise. I gave him a dollar. Others did the same, and I was told that he thus received quite a golden harvest.

The McLean House in Appomattox Courthouse, Virginia, with Union soldiers standing guard out front.

Edward Boykin served in the Confederate Army as a Lieutenant Colonel of the 7ᵗʰ Regiment of South Carolina Cavalry. This is the account[17] of his experiences on April 9, 1865, from early morning preparation for battle to the reception of his former enemy after the surrender.

The sun rose clear on this the last day, practically, of the Southern Confederacy. It was cool and fresh in the early morning so near the mountains, though the spring must have been a forward one, as the oak trees were covered with their long yellow tassels.

---

[17] Taken from *The Falling Flag: Evacuation of Richmond, Retreat and Surrender at Appomattox*, by Edward M. Boykin, 1874.

We gathered the brigade on the green on the Richmond side of the village, most of the men on foot, the horses not having come in. About eight o'clock a large portion of our regiment had their horses — they having been completely cut off the night before by the charge of Custar's cavalry on the turnpike, and were carried, to save them, into a country crossroad. Then the "Hampton Legion" got theirs. My impression is that the Twenty-fourth Virginia lost the most or a good many of their horses. The men built fires, and all seemed to have something to eat, and to be amusing themselves eating it. The woods on the southern and eastern side swarmed with the enemy and their cavalry — a portion of it was between us and the "James River," which was about twelve miles distant. General Fitz Lee's division of cavalry lay over in that direction somewhere; General Longstreet with General Gordon was in and on the outer edge of the town, on the Lynchburg side, and so we waited for the performance to commence.

Looking at and listening to the men you would not have thought there was anything special in the situation. They turned all the responsibility over to the officers, who in turn did the same to those above them — the captain to the colonel, the colonel to the brigadier, and so on.

…

About nine or ten o'clock, artillery firing began in front of General Longstreet, and the blue jackets showed in heavy masses on the edge of the woods. General Gary riding up, put everything that had a horse in the saddle, and moved us down the hill, just on the edge of the little creek that is here the "Appomattox," to wait under cover until wanted. Two of our young men, who had some flour and a piece of bacon in their haversacks, had improvised a cooking utensil out of a bursted canteen, and fried some cakes. They offered me a share in their meal, of which I partook with great relish. I then lay down, with my head, like the luxurious Highlander, upon a smooth stone, and, holding my horse's bridle in my hand, was soon in the deep sleep of a tired man. But not for long, for down came the general in his most emphatic manner—and those who know Gary know a man whose emphasis can be wonderfully strong when so minded. "Mount, men, mount!" I jumped up at the sharp, ringing summons with the sleep still in my eyes, and found myself manœuvring my horse with his rear in front. We soon had everything in its right place, and rode out from the bottom into the open field, about two hundred and fifty strong, to see the last of it.

Firing was going on, artillery and small arms, beyond the town, and there was General R.E. Lee himself, with Longstreet, Gordon, and the rest of his paladins.

When we rode into the open field we could see the enemy crowding along the edge of the woods — cavalry apparently extending their line around us. We kept on advancing towards them to get a nearer view of things, and were midway on the Richmond side between the town and a large white house with a handsome grove around it. In the yard could be seen a body of cavalry, in number about our own; we saw no other troops near. Two or three hundred yards to the right of the house an officer, apparently of rank, with a few men — his staff, probably — riding well forward, halted, looking toward the town with his glass. Just as he rode out General Gary had given the order to charge the party in the yard. Someone remarked that it looked like a flag of truce. "Charge!" swore Gary in his roughest tones, and on we went. The party in the yard were taken by surprise; they had not expected us to charge them, as they were aware that a parley was going on (of which, of course, we knew nothing), and that there was a suspension of hostilities.

We drove them through the yard, taking one or two prisoners — one little fellow, who took it very good-humoredly; he had his head tied up, having got it broken somewhere on the road, and was riding a mule. We followed up their retreat through the yard, down a road, through the open woods beyond, and were having it, as we thought, all our own way — when, stretched along behind the brown oaks, and moving with a close and steady tramp, was a long line of cavalry, some thousands strong — Custar's division — our friends of last night. This altered the complexion of things entirely; the order was instantly given to move by the left flank—which, without throwing our back to them, changed the forward into a retrograde movement.

The enemy kept his line unbroken, pressing slowly forward, firing no volley, but dropping shots from a line of scattered skirmishers in front was all we got They, of course, knew the condition of things, and seemed to think we did not. We fell back toward a battery of ours that was behind us, supported, I think, by a brigade of North Carolina infantry. We moved slowly, and the enemy's skirmishers got close enough for a dash to be made by our acting regimental adjutant—in place of Lieutenant Capers, killed the night before— Lieutenant Haile, who took a prisoner, but just as it was done one of our couriers — Tribble, Seventh regiment — mounted on a fine black horse, bareheaded, dashed between the two lines with a handkerchief tied upon a switch, sent by General Gordon, announcing the "suspension of hostilities."

By this time the enterprising adjutant had in turn been made prisoner. As soon as the orders were understood everything came to a stand-still, and for a while I thought we were going to have, then and there, a little inside fight on purely personal grounds.

An officer — a captain — I presume the captain in command of the party in the yard that we had attacked and driven back upon the main body — had, I rather expect, been laughed at by his own people for his prompt and sudden return from the expedition he had set out on.

He rode up at once to General Gary, and with a good deal of heat (he had his drawn sabre in his hand) wanted to know what he, Gary, meant by keeping up the fight after there had been a surrender. "Surrender!" said Gary, "I have heard of no surrender. We are South Carolinians, and don't surrender. [Ah! General, but we did, though.] Besides, sir, I take commands from no officers but my own, and I do not recognize you or any of your cloth as such."

The rejoinder was about to be a harsh one, sabres were out and trouble was very near, when an officer of General Custar's staff — I should like to have gotten his name — his manner was in striking contrast to that of the bellicose captain, who seemed rather to belong to the snorting persuasion — he, with the language and manner of a thorough gentleman, said, "I assure you, General, and I appreciate your feelings in the matter, that there has been a suspension of hostilities, pending negotiations, and General Lee and General Grant are in conference on the matter at this time."

His manner had its effect on General Gary, who at once sheathed his sabre, saying, "Do not suppose, sir, I have any doubt of the truth of your statement, but you must allow that, under such circumstances, I can only receive orders from my own officers; but I am perfectly willing to accept your statement and wait for those orders." (Situated as we were, certainly a wise conclusion.) Almost on the instant Colonel Blackford, of the engineers, rode up, sent by General Gordon, with a Federal officer, carrying orders to that effect.

We drew back to the artillery and infantry that were just behind us, and formed our battered fragments into regiments.

Desperate as we knew our condition to be since last night's affair, still the idea of a complete surrender, which we began now to see was inevitable, came as an awful shock. Men came to their officers with tears streaming from their eyes, and asked what it all meant, and would, at that moment, I know, have rather died the night before than see the sun rise on such a day as this.

And so the day wore on, and the sun went down, and with it the hopes of a people who, with prayers, and tears, and blood, had striven to uphold that falling flag.

It was all too true, and our worst fears were fully justified by the result. The suspension of hostilities was but a prelude to surrender, which was, when it came to a show of hands, inevitable.

General Lee's army had been literally pounded to pieces after the battle of "Five Forks," around Petersburg, which made the evacuation of Richmond and the retreat a necessity. When General Longstreet's corps from the north bank joined it, the "army of Northern Virginia," wasted and reduced to skeleton battalions, was still an army of veteran material, powerful yet for attack or defence, all the more dangerous from its desperate condition. And General Grant so recognized and dealt with it, attacking it, as before stated, in detail; letting it wear itself out by straggling and the disorganizing effect of a retreat, breaking down of men and material. The infantry were almost starved.

...

The terms of the surrender, and all about it, are too well known to go over in detail here — prisoners of war on parole, officers to retain side arms, and all private property to be respected, that was favorable to our cavalry, as in the Confederate service the men all owned their horses, though different in the United States army, the horses belonging to Government.

General Gary, true to the doctrine he had laid down in his discussion with the irate captain, that "South Carolinians did not surrender," turned his horse's head, and, with Captain Doby and one or two others, managed to get that night through the "cordon" drawn around us, and succeeded in reaching Charlotte, North Carolina, which became, for a time, the headquarters of the "Southern Confederacy" — the President and his Cabinet having established themselves there.

Colonel Haskell, who had been separated from us the night before, while gathering up the horses of the brigade, by the charge of cavalry on the turnpike, and had joined and been acting with General Walker and his artillery, came in about two o'clock. All the Confederate cavalry at Appomattox, some two thousand or twenty-five hundred, were under his command as ranking officer.

The brigade crossed the road and bivouacked in the open field near the creek, within a few hundred yards of the town. Our infantry, and what was left of the artillery, was scattered along the road for two or three miles toward Richmond — the enemy swarming in every direction around us, and occupying the town as headquarters.

...

General Lee was seen, dressed in full Confederate uniform, with his sword on, riding his fine grey charger, and accompanied by General Gordon, coming from the village, and riding immediately in front of where we were lying. He had not been particularly noticed as he had gone toward the town, for, though with the regiment, I have no recollection of his doing so. As soon as he was seen it acted like an electric flash upon our men; they sprang to their feet, and, running to the roadside, commenced a wild cheering that roused our troops. As far as we could see they came running down the hill sides, and joining in, along the ground, and through the woods, and up into the sky, there went a tribute that has seldom been paid to mortal man. "Faithful, though all was lost!"

The Federal army officers and men bore themselves toward us as brave men should. I do not recollect, within my personal observation, a single act that could be called discourteous — nor did I hear of one. On the other hand, much kindness and consideration were exhibited when circumstances made it warrantable — such as previous acquaintance, as was common among the officers of the old army, or a return of kindness when parties had been prisoners in our hands...

Regular rations were issued to men and horses.

...

Success had made them good natured. Those we came in contact with were soldiers — fighting men — and, as is always the case, such appreciate their position and are too proud to bear themselves in any other way. They, in the good nature of success, were more willing to give than our men, in the soreness of defeat, to receive.

The effect of such conduct upon our men was of the best kind; the unexpected consideration shown by the officers and men of the United States army towards us; the heartiness with which a Yankee soldier would come up to a Confederate officer and say, "We have been fighting one another for four years; give me a Confederate five dollar bill to remember you by," had nothing in it offensive.

The Final Story

For our final story, we will return to Union Private Theodore Gerrish. His account[18] of the final fight, surrender, and stacking of arms contains much of the soldier's experience. From privation to high comedy, and from jubilation to sad defeat, it is all here; a well written story...

It was the ninth of April, 1865, and our long march was drawing to a close. But a few men were in Company H, at nine o'clock that morning, and perhaps a portion of these, like the writer, were there because they promised us rations. Our column halted in a field, and our guns were stacked as if we were to remain for a time. The firing in our front which we had heard at intervals that morning seemed to have died away. We broke ranks, and a portion of the boys ran in search of water, and others for wood. I started on a double-quick, hoping to secure a fence rail for fuel, so that we could make coffee after our rations were issued. A thousand men were in the same field, and on the same business. I ran with all possible speed for a half mile, before I could secure one, and that, a huge oak rail, heavy enough for four men to carry. I managed to get the

---

[18] Taken from *Army Life: A Privates Reminiscences of the Civil War*, by Reverend Theodore Gerrish, 1882.

smaller end upon my shoulder, dragging the heavier, and slowly made my way to the regiment. It was all I could stagger under, and when I reached the company, great drops of perspiration were running down my cheeks. With an exclamation of triumph I threw down my load beside my comrades, but just at that moment the bugle blew "Fall in!" "Fall in!" The boys laughed loudly at my adventure, and advised me to take the rail along with me. To say that I was slightly disgusted does not express the situation.

Heavy firing was heard in our front, not over half a mile distant. Orders were given to double-quick. We dashed through a thick belt of woods, and met cavalrymen riding back, badly broken up and demoralized. They told us they had been fighting all night, and holding the rebels in check until we should arrive, and this explained why we had marched all night. We passed through the woods, and came out into a field some forty rods in width. For a fourth of a mile in our front there was flat and level ground, and then a ridge of land, on whose crest there was a house, barn, and numerous outbuildings. The field on either side, up to this hill, was bordered with a forest, while beyond, there was we knew not what. In that field we halted. A group of Union generals were sitting upon their horses near us Sheridan, Griffin, Chamberlain, and others. Sheridan was evidently much excited, and was talking rapidly, and adding emphasis to his words, by bringing his clenched right hand down on the open palm of his left. It was evident to all that some enterprise of importance was on foot. At that time we had but one man in Company H, who had any claims to piety, a grand fellow, quiet and beloved by all. He had marched all night, bound to keep up, but was so weak and footsore that he could hardly step.

When the company halted, and he saw Sheridan, he sank upon the ground with a comical groan of despair, and remarked, "The devil is to pay, sure!" And over beyond the hill, at about the same time, I think General Lee was cherishing the same opinion. Our brigade was quickly formed in two lines of battle to make a charge. Our regiment was in the front line, and General Sheridan formed a cavalry skirmish line in our front. The enemy's lines of battle were evidently over beyond the hill in our front, as some of their batteries opened upon us, and threw shot and shell very carelessly around. The skirmishers advanced at a round gallop, Sheridan leading them on. When they reached the crest of the hill, and entered the forest on our right, we advanced rapidly across the plain and climbed the hill. Just before we reached its top, a shell exploded in the barn, and in a moment it was in flames. In the confusion hens and chickens ran from the barn in every direction. By this time the enemy was pouring a very heavy artillery fire upon us, but it always requires something more than shot or shells to prevent hungry soldiers from chasing chickens, and so after the fowls we ran. Shells were crashing, officers were shouting for the men to keep in the ranks, the boys were screaming and laughing as they ran after the chickens, the flames roared and swept through the air, and the hens squalled in their most pathetic manner, as they were overtaken and captured. Altogether it was a most remarkable medley. When the poultry excitement subsided, and we all got back into the rapidly advancing line, and looked out in our front, our mirth quickly subsided.

It was a desperate situation one in which the most careless and indifferent would be brought to his senses. For three-fourths of a mile, an open field lay before us. A few rods of this distance was descending ground, then a level plain, and beyond that a ridge of land. At the foot of that ridge was the enemy's skirmish line. We could distinctly see the little rifle-pits in which they were intrenched. Beyond their skirmish line, and higher on the side of the hill, was their line of battle, behind breastworks, and back of this was their artillery, all in plain view. Their infantry had not opened fire upon us, but their artillery was firing rapidly and with good execution. We saw all this plainly, although advancing at a rapid rate. We well understood what our mission was to assault their position and silence their batteries. We thought of our comrades who had fallen out in the night, and who were then quietly sleeping back in the woods, and were angry with ourselves to think that for the hope of drawing rations we had been foolish enough to keep up, and by doing so, get in such a scrape. But it was then too late to fall out, and all we could do was to pull our hats down over our eyes as far as possible, keep up with the line, and endeavor to appear brave. We did not fear the artillery very much, for they fired over our heads, but dreaded the moment when the infantry should open on us. We descended the hill and advanced across the plain, and were not far from their skirmish line. Not many words were spoken, but every mind was busy. Like a flash we thought of all the past three years, so many dangers passed through, and here, after all these hardships and narrow escapes, just as the war was about to close, our regiment reduced to a hundred men, was hurled into this desperate position, where nearly all must be slaughtered. It did seem hard, but not a man in that little band flinched, and as coolly as we had ever marched upon the parade ground, we marched up to what we supposed was the gates of death. We saw a white object flutter in an orchard up in the rear of their line of battle. A signal for their infantry to open fire, growled the boys, as they saw it. Then we expected to see their line of battle mantled in fire and smoke as they poured volleys of death upon us; but a moment passed, and not a gun had been fired. We looked again; we saw the object we had supposed to be a signal flag, but it had changed its position. It was advancing almost down to their line of battle. It continued to advance, and passed their battle line. Three men accompanied it. What could it mean? It was a white flag. We could not believe our eyes. At a brisk gallop the officers rode to within twenty rods of our line, then turned down to our right where Sheridan had disappeared; and on we advanced. A staff officer came out from the woods; his spurs were pressed hard against the smoking flanks of his noble horse. He was swinging his hat like a madman, and yelling "Lee has surrendered! Lee has surrendered!" "Halt, halt, halt!" came the order, and the last charge was over. But such a scene! I cannot describe it. Seventeen years have passed, but the blood tingles in my finger tips now, as I think of it. There was such a change in the situation, such a transition in our experience! Men laughed and shouted, shook hands and actually wept for joy. Could it be possible? It seemed more like a dream. Had Lee actually surrendered, and was the war about to close?

The joy of that hour will never be forgotten. We forgot the long, weary marches, the hours of suffering, the countless exposures, and many sacrifices, and for the time, even forgot our disappointment in not drawing rations at nine o'clock that morning. Many of the boys were even then skeptical as to the actual surrender of Lee, and contended that he only sent in the flag of truce to gain time, and thus steal a march upon us; but in the afternoon all doubts were removed. The advanced lines of the enemy had been withdrawn soon after the white flag came within our lines, and now large numbers of the rebel soldiers came over to us. We were glad to see them. They had fought bravely, and were as glad as we that the war was over. They told us of the fearful condition General Lee's army was in, and we only wondered that they endured the hardships so long as they did. We received them kindly, and exchanged pocket knives and sundry trinkets, that each could have something to carry home as a reminiscence of the great event. To our division was assigned the honor of staying to receive the remainder of the arms, while the rest of the army moved back toward Richmond. We had three days' rations of food in our baggage wagons, and this was divided with our prisoners; and thus for the day or two intervening between the surrender and the final stacking of their arms, we camped on the same hillside, ate the same hard-tack, and almost drank from the same canteen. The rebels were all loud in their praise of General Grant, for the generous terms of the surrender, and pledged themselves to go home, and live and die under the shadow of the old flag. They had fought for four years, been completely whipped, were sadly disappointed, but, like men, were determined to go home and work to regain the fortunes they had lost.

For two days after the flag of truce came in, and hostilities ceased, we were making preparations for the formal surrender. We were very thankful that it was our privilege, at the close of the war, to witness this most important event, while all the army, save our division, marched back in the direction of Richmond.

The twelfth day of April, 1865, was a memorable one to the First division of the old Fifth army corps, for upon that day the army of General Lee stacked its arms, and the above named division was the one designated by General Grant to receive the surrender. The morning dawned clear and warm. At an early hour the regiments were prepared to fall into line. Major-General J. L. Chamberlain was in command of the brigade. Before nine o'clock the troops were in line, our brigade, consisting of nine old regiments, being in the advance. Anxiously we waited for the appearance of the rebel army. Soon we saw a gray column of troops advancing through the valley at our right. A thrill of excitement ran along the line, and exclamations like the following: "There they are," "The Johnnies are coming," "The Confederacy has found its last ditch," were whispered among the men. Before their advanced line reached our column, every man was in his proper position, and we stood like a blue wall at a "shoulder arms," as they marched in our front. There was a space of some four rods between us. When their column had advanced the length of our line, they halted, "front faced," and there we stood two hostile armies in well-formed lines, with only that narrow space between us. Our commander, with the true courtesy of a chivalrous spirit, gave the command "Shoulder arms," and we thus saluted our fallen enemies. They returned the salute, then "Ordered arms," "Fixed bayonets," "Stacked arms," placed their colors and equipments, upon the stacks thus made, moved by the "right flank," and marched sadly away. And thus they came and went, until all that remained of the grand old army of northern Virginia had stacked their arms. We had a most excellent opportunity to review these Southern troops, and notice their peculiar traits. As a rule they were tall, thin, spare men, with long hair and beard of a tawny red color. They were all clad in the uniform of Southern gray; nearly all were very ragged and dirty, while their broad-brimmed, slouching gray hats gave them anything but a soldierly appearance. A little fellow on my left, seeing how thin and lean they were, muttered, "No wonder we didn't kill more of them; either one of them would split a minie-ball if it should strike him."

...

Their arms were of all designs and patterns; many of them were of English make, and had been doubtless smuggled through the blockade by the English blockade runners. Their colors were all stained by storm, and many of them were torn to shreds; some were elegantly mounted upon richly ornamented staffs, while others were fastened to rough poles. It was quite an affecting scene to see some of the various color guards, as they were about to leave the old flags they had carried so long and defended so bravely, turn and tear small pieces from the old banner, and hastily put them in their pockets as if fearing our officers would forbid their doing it, if they saw them. Many a brave Southern soldier turned that day with tearful eyes from the old colors they had loved so well, and for which they had sacrificed so much. No conversation was allowed between the two armies as the surrender was being made, but occasionally a pleasant word would be exchanged. One division that we had encountered on several different fields of battle, halted in our front, and as they were stacking their arms they learned to what division we belonged, while one of them cried in a jocose manner: "Well, old fellows, we have met you again." And thus the day passed until they had all surrendered.

ABOUT THE AUTHOR

Mark Weaver, an amateur history buff, currently spends much of his time studying the American Civil War. In the course of his study, he has come across many amazing stories written by people who lived during the war, and he was inspired to collect some of the best into a book. That is how *War Stories* was born. Mark has also been collecting some of his favorite Civil War facts and stories on his website AmericanCivilWarStories.com.

Printed in Great Britain
by Amazon